D0044557

BACKLASH

BACKLASH

What Happens When We Talk Honestly about Racism in America

GEORGE YANCY

Foreword by Cornel West

ROWMAN & LITTLEFIELD
Lanham • Boulder • New York • London

Published by Rowman & Littlefield
A wholly owned subsidiary of The Rowman & Littlefield Publishing Group, Inc.
4501 Forbes Boulevard, Suite 200, Lanham, Maryland 20706
www.rowman.com

Unit A, Whitacre Mews, 26–34 Stannary Street, London SE11 4AB

Distributed by NATIONAL BOOK NETWORK

British Library Cataloguing in Publication Information Available

Library of Congress Cataloging-in-Publication Data

978-1-5381-0405-7 (cloth)
978-1-5381-0406-4 (electronic)

∞ ™ The paper used in this publication meets the minimum requirements of American National Standard for Information Sciences—Permanence of Paper for Printed Library Materials, ANSI/NISO Z39.48–1992.

Printed in the United States of America

CONTENTS

This book is dedicated
to all of those who are willing
to take the risk to love.

FOREWORD
The End of White Innocence

Cornel West

George Yancy is one of the few distinguished public philosophers willing to get his hands dirty in the muck and mire of white supremacy in
contemporary America. He possesses impeccable credentials in academic
continental and American philosophy, yet he also has chosen to intervene
in our escalating swamp of polarized discussions of racism. The age of
Trump—with its open neofascist presences, the collapse of civic public
discourse, and the increase of market-driven pundits—has promoted a
massive white backlash against any attempt to address the scope, depth,
and breadth of white supremacy.

This courageous book is a crucial form of fightback against the backlash.
Yancy's prophetic voice is a force for good in our "post-hope" era in which
"fake news" is most of the news, machismo poses and postures drown out
any "ethics of no edges," and rapacious narcissism undercuts any "ontology
of connectedness." Yancy gallantly tries to wrestle with what it means to be
human in a time in which vulgar and visceral dehumanization
predominates.

Like the inimitable James Baldwin, Yancy begins with tough love and
calls for the end of white innocence. This innocence is a kind of self-
delusion which denies vulnerability, risk, and reciprocity. It parades as an
insecure arrogance and willful ignorance that aides and abets crimes against

humanity. And let us not forget that white supremacy, like male supremacy and other horrific evils, is a crime against humanity. Just as the cowardly and vicious white supremacist backlash against Yancy's letter of tough love was a crime against him.

Ironically, Yancy begins with a strong critique of himself—of his own sexism and patriarchal socialization. Yet these crude and rude times have little space or patience for self-critique or irony. Instead, the avalanche of white hatred and contempt overflows and overwhelms Yancy's bid for understanding. His hermeneutical humility is toppled by hermeneutical breakdown. Yet he persists with a philosophical tenacity to get at the ugly truths of white supremacy. Needless to say, he pays a heavy cost—with dignity and determination.

My major challenge to Yancy's powerful and insightful text is that we get only small glimpses of what white maturity or white courage looks like. The supportive remarks of white readers for his brave words don't do justice to a long yet too thin tradition of white radicals who, like Yancy, risk their lives and careers for truth and justice. Nevertheless, this book is a brook of fire through which all of us must past.

ACKNOWLEDGMENTS

Thanks to Jon Sisk, vice president and senior executive acquisitions editor at Rowman & Littlefield, for sharing with me his powerful response when he first read Dear White America when it appeared at the *New York Times'* column, The Stone. I was honored by his response, one that was honest and heartfelt. His response came at a time when it was greatly needed. In the midst of the storm and crucible of such a magnitude of white racist responses, Jon's message functioned as a place of hope. I thank you for that, Jon. I also thank you for your encouragement that I rethink Dear White America in the form of a book. This was truly the impetus for bringing this book to fruition. I would also like to thank Kate Powers, assistant editor at Rowman & Littlefield, for all of her help with logistics, and her insight and professionalism. To Crystal Clifton, my copy-editor, thanks so very much for your insights, keen eyes, and thoroughness. The care with which you've worked on this book is much appreciated. And Elaine McGarraugh, senior production editor at Rowman & Littlefield, thanks for your wonderful assistance, enthusiasm for the book, and for making sure that I kept to the schedule.

A special thanks to philosopher Cornel West for writing the Foreword to this book. Cornel, I know that you are out there fighting the good fight, but you took the time to come through for your dear brother. Your voice, one grounded within a long and sustained prophetic tradition, is truly needed as America and the world spiral down into greater catastrophe and ruin. Yet your indefatigable hope convinces me to hold on and never allow despair to have the last word.

Thanks to philosopher Simon Critchley and editor Peter Catapano at the *New York Times*, cofounders of The Stone, who believe in the power of public philosophical discourse and dialogue. My work with Simon and Peter is a genuine honor. Peter's editorial work is brilliant. And his capacity for mutual understanding is greatly appreciated. So, to Simon and Peter, thanks for seeing the value in publishing the initial version of Dear White America. From the overwhelming and torrential response that it received, I have no doubt that we did something right, something momentous. Thanks for creating such a welcoming space to engage in public philosophy, especially at a time when the need for informed, critical, and honest dialogue about a range of deep political, ethical, global, and existential issues is under emboldened malicious and irresponsible attack from within "our" very nation.

Emma Clements, an editor par excellence, is to be thanked for her time, her expertise, and her meticulous editorial skills. She is one of the best editors with whom I've had the pleasure of working. Emma, thanks for what you do, and the powerful creative ingenuity that you possess.

I also thank Barbara Applebaum, Taine Duncan, Karen Teel, Maureen O'Connell, and Susan Hadley for all of their critical feedback and willingness to read over various chapters. Barbara, your friendship and profound pedagogical insights within the areas of critical whiteness studies and complicity pedagogy are deeply appreciated. Taine, your philosophical probing is deeply engaging and was instrumental in shaping important aspects of this book. Thanks for making time for my work, for grappling with my voice, for improving my insights. Karen, your thoroughness was amazing and helped to bring me to the finish line. Thank you for taking the time in giving so much of yourself. Maureen, thanks for making time to read through parts of this text. You immediately said yes when asked. For that I'm thankful. Susan, you read through the entire text, literally sitting with me going over, pouring over, the text in detail. You provided essential advice while, of course, respecting my philosophical voice, my style of engaging a concept, a word, a sentence. That can be a task. Thanks for honing my voice, especially when I metaphorically soared too close to the sun. What I needed was the smell of the earth as Adrienne Rich would demand. Thanks for keeping me grounded, honest, and true to my own philosophical aims within this text. Cassie Hill, a young philosopher on the rise, thanks for reading through the manuscript during a tight schedule. You are destined to be a philosopher who distinguishes herself.

A special thanks to bell hooks and the bell hooks Institute at Berea College for inviting me to engage in a wide-ranging conversation with an engaging audience of people concerned with eradicating injustice. I thank bell for her ceaseless effort to speak candidly when it comes to marking pain, suffering, and joy in this world. For those who may not know, bell's wit, humor, and show of hospitality are just amazing. Her friendship is warm and loving. Within this context, it was such an honor to participate in an engaged discussion about masculinity and other issues of social and philosophical importance with bell and the late Harry Brod at St. Norbert College in 2017. My condolences to Harry's life partner, Karen Mitchell. One of my favorite colleagues, Karlyn Crowley, who is an excellent scholar and director of the Cassandra Voss Center at St. Norbert College, is to be thanked for creating a space for the engaged discussion to take place. I would also like to thank Bettina Love for being there within that space and for her important work that critically engages the pedagogy of hip-hop.

Thanks to scholar Susannah Heschel for inviting me to give a public talk and engage with her students at Dartmouth College in late summer of 2017. I wrote an article titled "Is Your God Dead?" for the *New York Times'* column, The Stone, through the prism of the extraordinary work of Susannah's father, Rabbi Abraham Joshua Heschel. The objective of the article was to bring attention to the lack of religious and theological moral leadership in our contemporary moment. Susannah read the article and the rest was history. She is an engaging scholar and is unafraid to critique the multitudes of injustice manifest throughout our world. I am honored that we are friends.

Thanks to my colleagues John J. Stuhr and John Lysaker at Emory University. Stuhr, who was chair upon my arrival at Emory, is to be acknowledged for sharing a bit of the heat after the publication of Dear White America. And by this, I mean that he too, unfortunately, received some of the white supremacist nastiness sent my way. He, too, according to white supremacist logic, was to "blame," needed to be called vicious names, for playing a role in me being hired. Stuhr, thanks for standing tall and for your courage. Thanks for your leadership, collegiality, and friendship. Lysaker, now chair, also got to take part in reading some of the white supremacist hatred sent my way. Thanks for your voice in a time of need—a sane and brave voice. To the both of you, thanks for being allies during an unprecedented and difficult moment in my career as a philosopher, a public intellectual. It is during such times that friendships are needed.

Thanks to Emory University for being a prestigious institution that values the freedom of its scholars to speak with courage and daring.

I thank friend and colleague Anne Leighton for creating an indispensable petition on my behalf. Anne is also to be thanked for her fierce antiracist praxis. Anne has the kind of political integrity that is to be respected and envied. It has never been about the spotlight. I fear that she will balk at my thanking her here, but I must. So, there you have it. Thanks, Anne, for your principled stand on issues of tremendous importance to our very survival. I also thank the over one thousand individuals who supported me by signing the petition.

I thank the board of officers at the American Philosophical Association for their historic statement specifically against incidents of bullying and harassment of philosophers. Thanks for responding on my behalf and for all philosophers, especially those of us who critically engage different publics and who often come under attack through the publication of publicly "high profile" articles and essays. Thanks to the Committee on Public Philosophy and the Committee on the Status of Black Philosophers for drafting their supportive letter on my behalf and for their solidarity with me while I was under vicious verbal assault by white racist supremacist attacks and threats, especially of death and physical harm.

Thanks also to those international scholars and philosophers who read Dear White America and reached across space and time to show their support.

I would like to thank all of the white readers of Dear White America who decided to let go, even if for only a moment, of the proverbial mast of the ship and take a leap of faith, to listen to a voice different from your own, and accept the gift that Dear White America attempts to offer. Thanks for your honesty about your white racism, about the ways in which racism is subtle and systemic, and what that means for me, as a person racialized as Black, and for you, as a person racialized as white; indeed, what that means for this nation, the world. Thanks for being human, for aspiring to embrace a far more robust sense of relationality, for recognizing the ways in which there are no edges that separate us. And thanks for understanding that to thank you is not to "praise you," but it is to acknowledge your humility, vulnerability, and courage to take responsibility seriously, to desire a world that isn't broken, but whole.

James G. Spady is to be thanked for his continuous expressive genius even under especially difficult personal times. Man, you are an incredible human being.

I thank the Yancy boys. And thanks to the one Yancy girl of mine if you can hear me. Take a moment. Your father is fragile, he is finite, and he loves you with all of his heart. Dear White America was a gift to white people, but a risk. If you decide to emulate your father, know that some risks are worth taking. And as you take that risk, even though I might be long gone, which seems to be an existential contract impossible to break, know that my love for you is a constant. I want you to be brave, to speak with courage, and to leave love behind in a world that is filled with so much hate, violence, and divisiveness.

While this may come as a surprise, and, for some, inappropriate or perhaps undeserving, I would like to take this space to say something of importance *to* white supremacists. And while none of you are probably reading this book, one never knows. So, if I have your attention, take this to heart. In cosmic time, we are a blink, less than a blink. And while I have faith that there is more to all of this than this less-than-a-blink-moment, I am by no means certain. But let's assume that this is it, that someday, sooner or later for me and for you, we will become rotting corpses, that we (you and me) will never, ever come this way again, that death is the extinction of your consciousness and mine throughout all of eternity. As the universe expands and perhaps contracts again, what I'm saying is that we may never bear witness to being ever again. It seems to me that the weight of that alone ought to move you with a desperate ache to reach out to me, to desire to know me, to love me, because like you, I am not repeatable, we are both irreplaceable. The weight of that should disarm you. It should flood your body with passion, perhaps even tears, a form of suffering and sorrow that speaks to you of the sheer waste of time and effort that you put into making me your "enemy." Doing so defaces the miracle and mystery that we are, that we only have this less-than-a-blink-moment to get to know each other and possibly to love each other. I'm no hero. I don't want to be. But I know that my time is less than a blink and I'll be damned if I'm going to impair this moment, this less-than-a-blink-moment, that we have been gifted, hating you. It is so easy to hate. So, I'm asking for something complicated, something that is perhaps, at this moment, unknown to you, something whose beauty and promise will lay waste to what you think you are and of what you think you are capable.

INTRODUCTION

Talking about Racism: When Honesty Feels Like Too Much to Bear

I've always known that I'm not a nigger. But if I am not the nigger, and if it is true that your invention reveals you, then who is the nigger?

—James Baldwin

"Nigger!" "Nigger!" "Nigger!" "Nigger!" "Nigger!" "Nigger!" That and so much more vileness is the *backlash* that I had to contend with after many white people read my letter Dear White America that was published in the *New York Times'* column, The Stone, on December 24, 2015. That letter unearthed and exposed what, for me, I knew was there, but I had not dealt with on such a large scale, systematically and directly. At this point in my life, especially after so much *personal* white racist backlash, I am convinced that America suffers from a pervasively malignant and malicious systemic illness—white racism. There is also an appalling lack of courage, weakness of will, spinelessness, and indifference in our country that helps to sustain it. That indifference is itself a cruel reality, a reality that often makes me want to scream at the top of my lungs until I fall flat on my face from exhaustion. There were foul and nasty voice messages, sickening email messages, vulgar letters mailed to my university, and comments on many conservative and white supremacist websites[1] in which I was lambasted and called everything but a child of God. In retrospect, though, I was given a foreshadow. On one white supremacist website, there could have been others, in the same space that I was being berated and belittled, I noticed that there were already images glorifying Donald Trump. Staring at me, there was an image of his face right there, easily blending in with white supremacist maliciousness. I should have seen it coming.

Dear White America exposed the deep roots of American white supremacy and the subtle ways in which so many white people go about their daily lives oblivious to the gravity and violence of white racism in this country and the ways in which they simultaneously benefit from and contribute to that racism. *Backlash: What Happens When We Talk Honestly about Racism in America*, refuses to desist. The exposure continues; it must. Therefore, I remain relentless.

To open this book with the words that I have was not done in haste. I gave serious thought to whether I should open with such a repulsive, life-denying, and ugly racist epithet—"Nigger." Why give power, even if inadvertently, to white supremacist racism and its destructive discourse? My aim is certainly not to do that, but to lay bare the ugliness and violence of white supremacy in a concrete way. Why begin this book with a vicious white racist word that demeans and dehumanizes Black people; that spits white racist vitriol in my face and the faces of Black people? For those who might feel further traumatized by its use here, I apologize. Yet as Black people, within the context of the long history of white racist America, we have been perceived, constructed, and treated in ways that reduce our complex lives to that which white people have imagined us to be. And for so many of them, we are just that—niggers.

There are other concerns, too. Will this choice of opening turn away interested readers? I would hope not. Of course, the truth can be overwhelming. I refuse to tone it down. Am I using such an opening as a device to draw in readers, to stimulate readers' desire to read more, perhaps a crass maneuver to sell more books? Too much is at stake for crass self-interest, though you should continue to read, especially as America has failed miserably to have a serious and honest engaging conversation about race, one for which the aims ought to be to heal this nation.

And then there is my field, my vocation. I am a philosopher, I philosophize. I consider this book to be one that falls, though not exclusively, within the field of philosophy. The juxtaposition of the term "nigger" within the context of doing philosophy and being a philosopher feels, perhaps, to many, textually and conceptually cacophonous, incongruous. After all, such an opening is so out of step given philosophy's penchant for conceptual abstraction, where the messiness of the real world is left behind as theory soars unencumbered. Imagine the impact on philosophy books and philosophy courses whose central foci deal with ethics, aesthetics, social and political philosophy, or even metaphysics, were they to begin with the reality that in white America there is this contemptible category that white people created called "nigger." How would that impact ideal theory, the "purity" of philosophy, its evasions and obfuscations? What would such a beginning say about the racialized foundations of European and Anglo-American philosophy?

To open the book in this way wasn't easy. Like so many things in life, there is risk involved. I am willing to take that risk.

The truth can hurt, stun, unsettle, and unnerve. And yet, the truth must be told. So, call me a truth-teller, someone who dares to hold a disagreeable mirror up to you, white reader, and ask that you take a long and hard look without fleeing, running away, or seeing only what *you want to see*. I begin this book, therefore, with that ugliest of racist words to communicate to you in no uncertain terms that this is how I am seen in white racist America. Time is too short for equivocation. And despite what Donald Trump would have us believe, not all sides are to blame. Evasion comes at a price, one that is often deadly for those who suffer under white racist America. Perhaps you, white reader, have yet to hear the lower, though powerful and influential, frequencies all around you, and perhaps within you, that carry the horrid messages that deem my existence "sub-human," and for some, not human at all. And perhaps it is those messages that often trigger a response that can render me, and so many like me, dead.

That is the pain that I live with, that Black people live with here in white racist America. As Black people, we must reject the poisonous ideas that white America would rather we swallow, but that rejection, while necessary, isn't sufficient. That act of repudiation will not protect me from a white cop's bullets that are capable of penetrating the fragility of my Black body, leaving me dead. I become the victim, the casualty of white police violence because he or she "knows" that I'm a "criminal," "up to no good," a "nigger." So, this book opens, candidly, as a warning to Black America. We are not truly safe in America. Our relationship to this country, despite the profoundly beautiful ways in which we've shaped it into our own image, and demanded that it be true to its "scared" creeds, has always been one where we have been forced to lay claim to our humanity, to lay claim to it *ad nauseum*.

White reader, I ask that you at least attempt to tarry within the space of an existential burden, the burden of having to claim one's humanity, where one's humanity is the very condition for making such a claim at all. Yet that is my situation, that is the situation of Black people in white racist America, that truth is why I began with that ugly racist word, the word that attempts to deny me my humanity, the word that speaks to white racist America, its past and its present. By the way, there is nothing, absolutely nothing at all, that *assures* me that white America's collective future will be any different than a miserable failure when it comes to facing the existential necessity of addressing and eradicating white racism. For me, being within a situation where I need to justify my own humanity triggers feelings of pain, anger, and rage. There are other times when I'm trapped by a profound sadness. We have so little time on this earth to experience the deep mystery of being alive, of existing, of experiencing love, kindness, and gratitude. Yet there are so many who have chosen to dehumanize other human beings, to despise them, to marginalize them, to other them, to haunt them, to abuse them, to degrade them, to oppress them, to torture them, and to murder them. It is a sadness, though, that will never have the last word. Life moves forward and hopefully for the better despite the fact that so many would rather see that forward movement—that betterment—arrested.

These affective dimensions of pain, anger, and rage inform, they keep me alert. When it comes to white racism, they keep me one step ahead of those "good whites," so many like you, who disavow all white racist tendencies, racist assumptions, racist micro-aggressions, racist ways that you interact with me and other Black people on elevators, in stores, as we pass you by on the street, when you "see" us within your gated communities, when we walk next to your cars, ask you for direction. So, once again, to begin with the word "nigger" is to show you something about yourself—even if you have never used the word—about a social world that was created *for you*—not for me, perhaps never for me.

From my perspective, my chosen entry into this book captures part of the racist dynamics regarding the white "reception" of Dear White America. It points to deep embodied wounds suffered by Black bodies, and exposes deep layers of white America's psyche, its denials and color-evasions. Oh, and that one astonishing and repulsive lie—that we live in a postracial

America. Again, I want to scream; a scream that would lead to a collective Damascene-like conversion where your scales, white reader, fall from your eyes and where your very being is transformed, made anew, leaving white racism in its wake.

Immediately after penning Dear White America at the *New York Times'* column, The Stone, on December 24, 2015, on Christmas Eve, I was assaulted by a veritable massive deluge of callous, despicable racist epithets, "nigger" being the salient word of choice. White people woke up on Christmas morning, a day celebrated by millions of people around the world, to be reminded about their white racism, to jar their sense of being "innocent," to ask them for love in return for a gift. For those white readers of the letter who find nothing of religious significance about Christmas Eve or Christmas day, I guess that my letter came as a nuisance. Christmas, after all, is a vacation day, a day to take off from work. However, my letter was there asking for a different quality of labor, the labor of self-reflection, the labor of telling the truth. That kind of work requires a certain kind of energy, one that involves honesty and courage. For those white readers for whom Christmas Eve and Christmas day are the holiest of days, my letter was decidedly "unholy." I was there to remind them of what Rabbi Abraham Joshua Heschel writes, "We worry more about the purity of dogma than about the *integrity of love.*"[2]

In return, there was very little love shown toward me. There were white threats of physical violence, talk of putting a meat hook in parts of my body, threats of knocking my "fucking head off" (their words), of beating me and leaving me half dead, and vile demands that I kill myself immediately. And there was so much more. All of it speaks to a twisted racist logic emanating from a white racist American imaginary filled with anti-Black racism, and deep forms of hatred for me and people who look like me. The volume and systematic nature of the threats was unanticipated. Dear White America received over two thousand comments at The Stone, more than I had ever seen there. I was critiqued on YouTube.[3] I was invited to appear on Fox News and was contacted by numerous radio stations for interviews. All of these were vetted by my university so as to avoid sites motivated by spectacle and controversy. The piece was debated in classrooms. Professors unknown to me had their students urgently read the piece. At one high school, a teacher had his students read the piece and he shared their responses with me, which were respectful but not all in agreement with me. All that I had published prior to that piece took a back seat. When I was introduced to new colleagues, they would reference the piece. The piece had gone viral.

Dear White America had taken on a life of its own. My situation became so dangerous that it became necessary for me to contact campus police, and to share any and all racist messages sent to me. My university did its important and necessary part. I was encouraged by a message from the very top administrative layers of my university that my academic freedom was protected. Yet my predicament was not easy. Campus police had to monitor my office, periodically patrolling the floor on which my office is located. Departmental instructions were clear: no one was to provide any callers with my office hours. This felt like something from a fictional movie. This, however, was all too real. My chair and colleague at the time, John J. Stuhr, also began to receive ugly messages, implicating him in my hire. He became a "nigger lover." The intensity escalated. I needed to have police officers present at my invited talks at other universities. It all felt incredibly sur-real—dangerously so.

Every unfamiliar white face could have been one of those threatening racist violence. Such an experience leaves its mark, does its damage. The body begins to respond. I walked faster, looking around far more often, listening for suspicious sounds outside my office door. When there were knocks at my office door, I insisted that the person speak up and to do so clearly. Opening my office door to leave for the day took effort. One begins to think about additional forms of self-protection, specifically my Second Amendment right to self-defense. Look, there were white people who dem-onstrated unambiguous hatred toward me and were not reticent to speak of the use of violence against me. All of this was malevolent white racism. This was the stuff of history apparently "long gone," a lie that continues to breed profound levels of denial and pervasive racist injustice.

In response to all of the racist reactions, colleague and ally Anne Leigh-ton created an important petition on my behalf. She didn't mince words, "Philosopher George Yancy is currently under attack (receiving racist hate mail and threats of violence) as the author of 'Dear White America.'"[4] In the petition, she called upon the American Philosophical Association (APA) to display the "letter of support/petition prominently on its website and distribute it to its membership."[5] She was also clear regarding the target that she had in mind. She wrote, "I am not asking this out of a liberal respect for intellectual freedom. I am asking this out of a rejection of and a disdain for racism."[6] Over one thousand people signed the petition. Soon after, the board of officers at the APA, citing Dear White America as a catalyst, released a historic statement specifically against incidents of bullying and harassment of philosophers. The statement was written by both the Committee on Public Philosophy and the Committee on the Status of Black Philosophers. While I would have liked to have seen a more direct and engaged condemnation of white supremacy as such, the APA did show its support. I was also deeply moved by sixty-eight philosophers and public intellectuals who came out against an attempt to silence me. "We stand together in support of our colleague George Yancy," they wrote, "and strongly repudiate these attempts to silence him."[7]

In many ways, the book that you hold in your hands provides an urgent contemporary narrative, just one of many, of what it means to be embodied as Black and to be the target of white racist hatred. It is also a window into the life of a Black philosopher who believes that the practice of philosophy, the love of wisdom, must speak to those who formally reside outside of the classroom and the academy. It is the ugly truth regarding the price to be paid for daring to speak courageously within the context of a variety of public spaces. This book also speaks to the deep pathology of racism, the disease of white racism, and how it has proven ineradicable thus far. And it speaks to the damn near impossibility of having an honest discussion with white people about white racism, *their white racism*. At the end of the day, not only do they not see my pain and suffering, Black pain and suffering, they don't really see us, see me. How does one speak truth to those who refuse to see you, to hear you? How does one speak truth when what you have to say is in some sense not even *hearable*? And the responses have not yet ceased. As recently as July 30, 2017, I received this message:

> What a moron. You're the racist. Why don't you stop wasting your time on this race baiting bullshit and go be a hero and save your ghetto neighborhoods where blacks are shooting each other by the hundreds. Pendejo!

And on August 17, 2017:

> I am white, AMERICAN non-racist, not [a] bigot. You are a racist PIG. You are the reason for much of the problems in this country. You and pigs like al sh(it)arpton, jessie (I never had a job) jackson, spike (if I was white none of

my movies would have been anything). Show your face and I'll debate your sorry ass.

As I will remind you, white reader, throughout this book, Dear White America was intended as a gift and for which I asked for love in return, love from white people, love from your white brothers and sisters. I know love when I see it. And I also know something about the *absence* of love, where there is a kind of indifference. The ruthless white racist responses directed toward me in response to Dear White America, many of which I share and critically engage throughout this book, I have come to know firsthand. I know what the unmitigated *presence* of white hatred looks like, feels like.

"'Dear White America': Another uppity nigger thinks it has the right to lecture Whites."

"Blame your parents who made you Black. White America had nothing to do with it."

It is easy to dismiss these and so many other white racist responses that I share throughout this book as the product of a few white supremacist "fringe" groups. You know, the "really bad" whites, like the Ku Klux Klan, the neo-Nazis, and other white supremacists such as those within the alt-right movement. As should now be indelibly fixed into American consciousness, these were the people who came to rally in Charlottesville, Virginia, on August 12, 2017, in protest of the planned removal of a Confederate statue representing General Robert E. Lee. They were clearly identifiable white supremacists, carrying torches, Confederate flags, and guns at the "Unite the Right" rally. America and the world got to hear racist chants such as "Blood and Soil"[8] and "Jews will not replace us."[9] It was within that tragic white supremacist space that a white woman, thirty-two-year-old Heather Heyer, was tragically killed by a white supremacist who drove his car into a crowd of protesters. And while we *must* all grieve the loss of Heyer, we must not forget the history of white supremacy, white terror, and white brutalization that Black people have suffered for centuries, those scenes of white bloodlust and white hatred. We must not forget the ways in which Black bodies are considered in our contemporary moment to be "surplus" bodies, "disposable" bodies, "nigger" bodies. When I think about the rally that took place in Charlottesville, Virginia, there is no doubt about how I am seen and how Black people are seen by those same white supremacists. I know how they brutally beat twenty-year-old Black male DeAndre Harris with metal poles in a parking lot in Charlottesville, Virginia. Some have said that the racist brutality that took place will leave a permanent stain in Charlottesville, Virginia. America has already been indelibly stained with the blood of innocent Black bodies and bodies of color who have suffered and continue to suffer from the violence of white supremacy. And we must never forget Indigenous peoples in North America who were decimated by American whites.

Black people are painfully aware of white America's centuries-old *damnable* history of anti-Black racism and the fact that Black Americans, despite our approach of the third decade of the twenty-first century, continue to struggle over what America means in terms of functioning as a place called "home." White America, as a whole, has never been hospitable toward Black people, but hostile to our very *being*. Being Black in white America has always raised the question of the validity and legibility of our existence, or, more accurately, when engaging the existential predicament of Black people in white America, "there is a zone of nonbeing."[10]

I did not expect Trump to understand the existential and ethical magnitude of this zone of nonbeing. I did not expect him to address its anti-Black vileness. In fact, he did the opposite. He gave support to it. We must never, ever, forget that when Trump did speak about the white supremacist violence that occurred in Charlottesville, Virginia, his words were perfunctory and deeply problematic. He said, "We condemn in the strongest possible terms this egregious display of hatred, bigotry, and violence on many sides, on many sides."[11] How many sides were there? The white supremacists are those who hate. Their agenda, their racist philosophy, is predicated on hate. Their very identities are founded upon self-avowed white racist beliefs and practices. They are anti-Black racists and anti-Semites, among many other things. They are the ones who believe that, as Black, I am not fit to live, that Black people are not fit to live, and that Jews are not fit to live. That is the side that Trump morally equated with the antiracist opposition, which was the other side. I fail to see the "many sides" of violence when only one side is the very embodiment of white supremacist hatred and violence.

After two full days, Trump's voice lacked moral conviction, ethically weak and destitute. Trump's voice was orchestrated through a teleprompter. His words seemed forced, as if those around him needed to correct the record, to make him look morally committed, more "presidential," in ways that he failed to do or is incapable of doing on his own initiative. In fact, it was more like moral rhetoric under pressure, not the real stuff of moral conviction. The real Trump is the one who dared to argue that the white supremacists in Charlottesville, Virginia, are morally equivalent to those who came to resist and protest against the white supremacists. For Trump, "there's blame on both sides."[12] Trump is guilty of moral forfeiture, a loss of moral authority when it comes to race relations in this country. Then again, "loss" implies that there was moral authority regarding race relations to begin with. Truth be told, for Trump, he had no moral authority regarding race from the beginning. And it is not just Trump's "belligerent approach to race relations"[13] that is the problem. It is his appalling ignorance of the complex history of race relations in this country. Then again, perhaps that history is of little or no concern to him. In other words, perhaps he is all too aware of what he is doing. In that case, he doesn't give a damn about being on the right side of history as he already thinks that the "right side of history" is American white nativism, an approach that solidifies his white supremacist sensibilities and his political base. The "right side of history," for Trump, is whichever side he selfishly, irrationally, and viciously chooses. What more evidence do we need? Well, what about referring to NFL protesters, typically African Americans, as sons of bitches? At a rally in support of Senator Luther Strange in Alabama, Trump said, "Wouldn't you love to see one of those NFL owners, when somebody disrespects our flag, to say, 'get that son of a bitch off the field right now, out, he's fired. He's fired!'"[14] This is not just the disrespect of First Amendment rights, which is indicative of Trump's authoritarianism, but it is profoundly disrespectful, foulmouthed, nasty, and dehumanizing toward the players and their mothers. The last time I checked, a bitch is a female dog. This is not just an attack on the constitutionality of protest as the exercise of free speech, but a vicious attack against the precious mothers of those NFL players. To that I say, kneel in droves and keep on kneeling until Black people in this country are treated with respect and are no longer the targets of white racist violence, including the discursive violence perpetrated by Trump and others who don't give a damn about Black lives. Trump has ushered in unadulterated *evil*, an expression that I rarely use. Sadly, and perhaps tragically, this is probably only the beginning.

America has abysmally failed to have an honest and critical conversation about race. This conversation continues to be crushed from occurring under Trump's leadership. While he didn't create the problem of white supremacy, his moral ineptitude and white nativist strategic positioning are such that he contributes to deeper levels of suffering and division within this country. We are at a dangerous moment in American history; hell, world history.

What happened in Charlottesville, Virginia, was nasty, ugly, disturbing, and violent. In fact, what happened was spectacularly so. It is the *spectacular* dimensions of white supremacy that makes it easy and convenient for "good whites" to distance themselves from the "bad ones," the self-avowed white supremacists. There is no moral equivocation here, though. I recognize the antiracist forms of resistance which white brothers and sisters engage in. That cannot be disputed. What I would ask is that white people in droves come out against their own white racism, the nonspectacular kind, the everyday kind, the kind that Black people and people of color continue to experience, though not necessarily at the end of a metal pole.

Barbara Applebaum writes that white people must be aware of "the ways in which power circulates through all white bodies in ways that make them directly complicit for contributing to the perpetuation of a system that they did not, as individuals, create."[15] And Paul Waldman writes:

> As a white person, I'll continue to enjoy this [white] privilege almost no matter who I am or what I do. In my heart I could be the most kind-hearted humanitarian or the most vile sociopath. I could be assiduously law-abiding or a serial killer. I can dress in a suit or in torn jeans and a hoodie, and no one will react to me with fear or suspicion, because if they don't know me they will assume they know nothing. I am myself, nothing more or less. That's privilege.[16]

It is that white privilege that has implications for my Black body. You see, to be Black in America is to be always already *known*, and white people assume that they know *everything* about me.

In Dear White America, I acknowledge that you may have never used the N-word in your life, and that you may hate the KKK. Yet this does not mean that you don't harbor white racism and benefit from white racism. As a white person, you are part of a system that allows you to walk into stores where you are not followed, where you go for a bank loan and your skin color does not count against you, where you don't need to engage in "the talk" that Black people and people of color must engage in with their children so that they might live for another day. And it is as you reap comfort from being white that we suffer for being Black and people of color. This is how we are tied to each other. You see, your comfort is linked to our pain and suffering. Just as my comfort in being male is linked to the suffering of women, which makes me sexist, so, too, you are racist. I know that this is hard to hear, because so many of you have this limited understanding of what white racism looks like. For you, white reader, it is exclusively what happened in Charlottesville, Virginia. However, from you, white reader, to the extent to which you are capable, I ask for greater depth of understanding, courage, compassion, and love.

There are times when I watch CNN discussions regarding race and racism in America and there are three or four Black pundits who have been invited to talk about race. Within this context, the host, say, Anderson Cooper, has on his show such Black political analysts as Van Jones, Symone Sanders, Bakari Sellers, or Angela Rye. Here is the problem, and here is where talking about race and the honesty thereof feels like it's too much to bear. The likelihood of Jones, Sanders, Sellers, or Rye finding themselves in a situation where they are directly confronted by the likes of those white supremacists in Charlottesville, Virginia, is unlikely. Yet highly likely, guaranteed even, is the fact that they will undergo everyday forms of white racism at the hands of those white people who would never identify with white supremacy. While Anderson Cooper and his Black pundits, or Don Lemon and his white pundits, will agree that white supremacy is unacceptable and morally abhorrent, the Black pundits will not call Cooper out on his white privilege and power, and Lemon will not call out his white pundits on their white privilege and power. Within white America, Cooper's life, its value, its immunity to certain forms of racial harm, is granted a different value than that of, say, Lemon's Black life.

It is that difficult conversation that we must have; it is that form of telling the truth about race that we continue to avoid, that white people especially continue to avoid. That is what Dear White America speaks to. That is the gift that I want you to accept, to embrace. It is a form of knowledge that is taboo. Imagine the impact that the acceptance of this gift might have on you, white reader, and the world; imagine Anderson Cooper telling the world that, "I, too, am racist. And while not part of the KKK, I, too, perpetuate white supremacy because I benefit from a white racist systemic structure to which I'm embedded and in terms of which Black people and people of color suffer." That is the scary work to be done. That is what Dear White America asked of white readers.

I approached writing this book as a philosopher. Philosophy raises questions that are existentially heavy to bear. This book certainly does that. Furthermore, throughout this book, my identity as a philosopher is communicated. This I take to be something to be expected. In fact, to repress completely that identity would mean erasing a very significant part of who I am that I treasure. However, I am first and foremost a human being, a vulnerable and suffering human being. While it is true that philosophy is my vocation, in fact, a deep calling and a deep urge, you and I, white reader, possess our humanity in common despite the history of white supremacy denying me mine, and despite the history of white *terror* which belied and belies my humanity and the humanity of Black people.

While I speak in a certain philosophical register, this is not meant to be alienating or condescending. I say this because I realize that some white readers will think that my choice of words and metaphors are designed to either prove something about my "intellectual sophistication" or subtly communicate something about their "ignorance." This is not my intention. I'm not trying to philosophically grandstand. What I'm doing throughout the book as a whole is a way of offering you, white reader, a way to engage in a deeper self-understanding of what it means to be white from a perspective outside your self-understanding, a place that is closed off or where you have created an edge beyond which my voice and my presence are not welcome. So, if the language that I use fails to communicate that sense of a mutually shared and vulnerable conversation, a sense of relational suffering, then I accept that as my fault. And for those who see these qualifications as concessions to white people, to white power, then you've missed what is at stake. Know that the lives of my Black sons, and the lives of Black people, are at stake within the belly of this beast called white supremacist America. I seek white people, flawed though they are within the context of understanding and struggling to trouble, confront, and "undo" their whiteness, who long for genuine human relationality, a conception of the human that transcends whiteness as the very expression of the human. I'm in search of those white people who are committed to achieving a postwhite racist humanity, those who are prepared to live a life of love that demands the pain of truth-telling and the radical possibility of being truly human. I know that you didn't ask for this letter, but acts of generosity in the form of gift-giving are often unasked.

It is a greater sense of genuine relationality that I seek. It is that seeking that is behind my gift. It is a very real desire for genuine human connection, not something that is just non-violent, but that which dares to resist white supremacy's effort to keep us from loving each other, being truthful to each other. This honest conversation about race is one that each of us must enter into from where we are. This is, in fact, what is required. It is a place of genuine human relationality that I seek.

My sense is that what many white people don't see, and what I'm courageously trying to suggest, is that it's worth experiencing pain, loss, and disorientation in order to connect across the color line, perhaps to undo that line forever. White reader, I long for robust forms of ethical connection. *Backlash* arises from that longing. And my hope is that you don't read this book as my looking for self-gratification of watching you squirm. That is a waste of time, a waste of *my* time. And while profound discomfort is necessary given the weighty ethical and existential issues at stake here, there is no pleasure on my part to be gotten from self-indulgence. *Backlash* is about rethinking how we relate to each other. It is about how we will either rise together or how we will fall together. Yet because whiteness as a structure of power and privilege has been on your side, both nationally and globally, there is differential labor to be performed. And you'll have to do the lion's share of it, which means that you will need a bigger heart, a greater tenacity to get to know us on *our terms*, to respect us on *our terms*, and possibly to love us on *our terms*, where that love is preceded by the process of laying bare the truth about your whiteness, and engaging in processes of deep structural transformation that create material conditions that belie whiteness as a systemic hegemonic feature of American social, political, economic, cultural, and epistemic life. And just as you are required to do the lion's share, I am more than prepared to hold up that disagreeable mirror lest your act of truth-telling (and heavy lifting) falls back into an intolerable form of white narcissism, or "white innocence," or perhaps even white "nobility" and white paternalism.

Backlash is about taking risks, vulnerability, and growth. Because of this, "white innocence" must be dispensed with at the proverbial gate. *Backlash*, however, is a gift that encourages telling the truth about your white self to the extent to which that is possible. It is a gift that disorients, and where, if taken seriously, you will be prepared to admit to what Heschel calls "the *monstrosity of* [racial] *inequality*," the monstrosity of denial that you engage in when it comes to the everyday poisonous effects of your white racism, the monstrosity of your dishonesty when it comes to Black pain and suffering because of your white privilege and power, and the monstrosity of how white bodies are differentially regarded and valued in relationship to Black bodies and bodies of color. *Backlash* offers a new vision, a radically different way for you, white reader, to see, to relate, to be. As James Baldwin reminds us, "People who shut their eyes to reality simply invite their own destruction, and anyone who insists on remaining in a state of innocence long after that innocence is dead turns himself into a monster."

A POSTSCRIPT TO THE INTRODUCTION

White reader, please know that those monsters to which Baldwin refers are all too real, all too threatening, all too deadly. They continue to haunt. I had no plans to write a postscript to the introduction. However, just days before receiving the copyedited version of *Backlash*, the haunting began again. On November 11, 2017, I received a letter that was sent to my university mailbox. The actual letter was handwritten on both sides in black ink on a sheet of paper torn from a legal pad, the kind with yellow colored sheets. The envelope looked familiar, especially as I had seen others that carried letters of white racist vitriol. There was no return address. Even as I, at this moment, have removed the letter out of its envelope, the letter feels dirty to the touch, nasty, contaminated with hatred. Each time that I've touched it, as I must do now for purposes of typing it word-for-word, I wash my hands afterward. There is a sense of needing to wash away the written filth. Yet there is also that sense of being careful, of wondering just what was smeared on the letter—feces or perhaps other bodily fluids. Paranoia? I don't think so. This is justified fear in a white supremacist America where my very being is hated, degraded, and seen as the "object" of all manner of unconscionable white racist behavior.

Dear Mr. Yancy, I am writing to you to voice my displeasure with what you said about WHITE PEOPLE. You claim that all White people are Racists! Really now? You, sir are one to talk!! You sound just like the following Racists. Here is a list of who I mean. They're Al Sharpton, Oprah Winfrey, Whoopi Goldberg, Spike Lee, Samuel L. Jackson, Bill Cosby, Danny Glover, Harry Belafonte, Movie Director John Singleton, Shannon Sharpe, Scottie Pippen (former NBA player), Rappers Ice Cube, Chuck D., Flavor Flav, DMX, and Snoop Dogg; former MLB players Carl Everett, Ray Durham and Hall of Famer Hank Aaron! When I read what you said about White people, I was like this guy is a total lowlife Racist piece of shit! It's so true! You are an asshole! You deserve to be punished with several fists to your face! You're nothing but a troublemaker! You need to really "Get a life!" I've had enough of your Racist talk! You'd better watch what you say and to whom you say it! You may just end up in the hospital with several injuries or maybe on a cold slab in the local morgue! I wouldn't be surprised if you've gotten several Death Threats! You're inviting trouble when you accuse the entire White Race of being Racists! You've got a big mouth that needs to be slammed shut permanently! I'm not going to give you the opportunity to find out who I am. Good luck with that! By the way, this letter I'm sending you is certainly not a Death Threat! I could've done that, but that's not me! I'm tired of your Racist kind!

As I have provided in-depth analyses of the racist comments sent to me or directed at me in subsequent chapters, I will not spend a great deal of time on this one. However, I want you, white reader, to know that the backlash continues. There are aspects of this letter, however, that must be addressed. Notice how the white writer names only prominent Black people, and does so across a wide range of areas, from politics, to entertainment, to sports. One wonders if the writer knows any other Black people. One wonders if the writer has had any real and meaningful contact with Black people in his/her daily life. This point would be silly to pose were it not true that white people, for the most part, possess the privilege of deciding to remain within all white social spaces, spaces where Black people are de facto excluded. And what exactly do Flavor Flav and Oprah Winfrey have in common? Well, let's see. Oh, both are Black. And what, pray tell, does the writer mean by "racism" or what it means to be a racist? The writer offers absolutely no explanation, no definition, and no analysis. I don't recall a time in world history when African nations divided up Europe to be possessed by force. There was no "African Berlin Conference"[17] that involved the "legitimate" scramble and control of Europe. I don't recall white people being sold into slavery by Black people in power. I don't recall white people being chained to the bottom of slave ships only to be carried far off to have their bodies exploited, viciously beaten, raped, burned, castrated, lynched, and made to hate their bodies and those who looked like them. Black people have not benefited from "Black privilege" because of some fictive notion of pervasive, systemic, and institutional Black power.

Obviously, the writer has neither read me correctly nor bothered to openly discuss with me what I mean by the term racism. Without any defense of what constitutes a racist or racism, except for simply dropping names, the writer argues that I am a racist and the Black people that have been identified are racists. I have become the quintessential so-called racist because I refuse to let white people off the proverbial hook by not speaking truth to the ways in which they reap benefits from their whiteness and how they thereby perpetuate white supremacy and white power; indeed, how they are complicit with white supremacy. Yet the white writer speaks as if he/she is a victim of racist oppression. And for this I am a "total lowlife Racist piece of shit!" And I ought to fear that I may "end up in the hospital with several injuries." And then the threat intensifies—"or maybe on a cold slab in the local morgue!" And I apparently have a big "mouth that needs to be slammed shut permanently." White reader, please tarry with these words. My life has just been threatened. Read it again! Feel it! Drink it in! This white person's response, and so many more responses of other white people that I will share within this book, fantasizes about harm done to me, my death. The white writer then belies what he/she intends by denying that the letter is a death threat. And then notice the white arrogance: "I could've done that." Sorry, but I'm not thankful for anything here. The letter *is a death threat*, it is abhorrent, mean-spirited, and sickening. The writer also teases me within the context of the threat: "I'm not going to give you the opportunity to find out who I am. Good luck with that!" In truth, I have absolutely no desire to find out who this white writer happens to be. So, there is no "good luck with that." The writer does communicate something here that is quite revealing, though. The writer implies that he/she could be someone that I see every day, who I walk by, greet, or even teach. You see, that is part of the mendacity of whiteness. All the smiles, the eye contact, and the social spaces of interaction—and yet, there I am, just a "nigger" to you, a Black body lying dead on a cold slab for daring to speak the truth. It is indeed a crime to think as a Black person in white America. It is a war waged against critical thought itself.

After receiving the letter, I decided to share it with my students in my graduate philosophy seminar. We had been discussing race and embodiment. So, the conceptual space was ripe. I wanted a witness. No, I *needed* a witness. I think that I wanted my students to help carry some of what I was feeling. So, I read it aloud. I had not anticipated my emotional response. As I read the letter, I began to feel a different kind of threat. The kind of threat that has implications for those whom I love. You see, white reader, a threat to my life will inevitably impact the lives of my loved ones. And that is a threat that impacts me, my body, my spirit, with a different kind of gravitas. Completing the letter, I looked at my students as I thought about the reverberations of such a threat. My eyes watered, my body became stilted, I felt a rush of unspeakable anger run through my blood. "This involves my loved ones. I can't take this shit anymore! I need a few minutes outside of class." Silence pervaded the classroom space. Looking back, I wish that I had said, "Fuck it all! It is not worth it. White people will never value my humanity. White America will never be honest about its hatred of Black bodies. So, let's end this class session on that. Let's just say, 'Fuck it all.'" Well, that didn't happen. I came back into the room, where everyone was still silent. My students' faces, for the most part, were turned down. I know what they had felt, Black students, students of color, and white alike. They bore witness to my vulnerability, my suffering. And they saw the impact within an otherwise safe academic space. A few moments passed, I apologized, and I resumed teaching. The space between us within that classroom was not the same; *we* witnessed something together. That space will never be the same.

1

THE LETTER: DEAR WHITE AMERICA[1]

Dear White America:

I have a weighty request. As you read this letter, I want you to listen with love, a sort of love that demands that you look at parts of yourself that might cause pain and terror, as James Baldwin would say.[2] Did you hear that? You may have missed it. I repeat: *I want you to listen with love*. Well, at least try. We don't talk much about the urgency of love these days, especially within the public sphere. Much of our discourse these days is about revenge, name calling, hate, and divisiveness. I have yet to hear it from our presidential hopefuls, or our political pundits. I don't mean the Hollywood type of love, but the scary kind, the kind that risks not being reciprocated, the kind that refuses to flee in the face of danger. To make it a bit easier for you, I've decided to model, as best as I can, what I'm asking of you. Let me demonstrate the vulnerability that I wish you to show. As a child of Socrates, James Baldwin, and Audre Lorde, let me speak the truth, refuse to err on the side of caution.

This letter is a gift for you. Bear in mind, though, that some gifts can be heavy to bear. You don't have to accept it; there is no obligation. I give it freely, believing that many of you will throw the gift back in my face, saying that I wrongly accuse you, that I am too sensitive, that I'm a race hustler, and that I blame white people (you) for everything. In response to other articles that I have written, I have read many of your comments. I have even received some hate mail. In this letter, I ask you to look deep, to look into your souls with silence, to quiet that voice that will speak to you of your white "innocence." So, as you read this letter, take a deep breath. Make a space for my voice in the deepest part of your psyche. Try to listen. Practice being silent. There are times when you must quiet your own voice to hear from or about those who suffer in ways that you do not.

What if I told you that I'm sexist? Well, I am. Yes. I said it and I mean just that. I have watched my male students squirm in their seats when I've asked them to identify and talk about their sexism. There are few men, I suspect, who would say that they are sexists, and even fewer would admit that their sexism actually oppresses women. Certainly not publicly as I have just done. No taking it back now.

To make things worse, I'm an academic, a philosopher. I'm supposed to be one of the "enlightened" ones. Surely, we are beyond being sexists. Some, who may genuinely care about my career, will say that I'm being too risky, that I am jeopardizing my academic livelihood. Some might even say that as a Black male, who has already been stereotyped as a "crotch-grabbing, sexual fiend," I'm at risk of reinforcing that stereotype. (Let's be real, that racist stereotype has been around for centuries; it is already part of white America's imaginary landscape.)

Yet, I refuse to remain a prisoner to the lie that we men like to tell ourselves—that we are beyond the messiness of sexism and male patriarchy, that we don't oppress women. Let me clarify. This doesn't mean that I intentionally hate women or that I desire to oppress them. It means that despite my best intentions, I perpetuate sexism every day of my life. Please don't take this as a confession for which I'm seeking forgiveness. Confessions can be easy, especially when we know that forgiveness is immediately forthcoming.

As a sexist, I have failed women. I have failed to speak out when I should have. I have failed to engage critically and extensively their pain and suffering in my writing. I have failed to transcend the rigidity of gender roles in my own life. I have failed to challenge those poisonous assumptions that women are "inferior" to men or to speak out loudly in the company of male philosophers who believe that feminist philosophy is just a non-philosophical fad. I have been complicit with, and have allowed myself to be seduced by, a country that makes billions of dollars from sexually objectifying women, from pornography, commercials, video games, to Hollywood movies. I am not innocent.

I have been fed on a poisonous diet of images that fragment women into mere body parts. I have also been complicit with a dominant male narrative that says that women enjoy being treated like sexual toys. In our collective male imagination, women are "things" to be used for our visual and physical titillation. And even as I know how poisonous and false these sexist assumptions are, I am often ambushed by my own hidden sexism. I continue to see women through the male gaze that belies my best intentions not to sexually objectify them. Our collective male erotic feelings and fantasies are complicit in the degradation of women. And we must be mindful that not all women endure sexual degradation in the same way.

I recognize how my being a sexist has a differential impact on Black women and women of color who are not only victims of racism, but also sexism, *my sexism*. For example, Black women and women of color not only suffer from sexual objectification, but the ways in which they are objectified is linked to how they are racially depicted, some as "exotic" and others as "hyper-sexual." You see, the complicity, the responsibility, the pain that I cause runs deep. And, get this. I refuse to seek shelter; I refuse to live a lie. So, every day of my life I fight against the dominant male narrative, choosing to see women as subjects, not objects. But even as I fight, there are moments of failure. Just because I fight against sexism does not give me clean hands, as it were, at the end of the day; I continue to falter, and I continue to oppress. And even though the ways in which I oppress women are unintentional, this does not free me from being responsible.

If you are white, and you are reading this letter, I ask that you don't run to seek shelter from your own racism. Don't hide from your responsibility. Rather, begin, right now, to practice being vulnerable. Being neither a "good" white person nor a liberal white person will get you off the proverbial hook. I consider myself to be a decent human being. Yet, I'm sexist. Take another deep breath. I ask that you try to be "un-sutured." If that term brings to mind a state of pain, open flesh, it is meant to do so. After all, it is painful to let go of your "white innocence," to use this letter as a mirror, one that refuses to show you what you want to see, one that demands that you look at the lies that you tell yourself so that you don't feel the weight of responsibility for those who live under the yoke of whiteness, your whiteness.

I can see your anger. I can see that this letter is being misunderstood. This letter is not asking you to feel bad about yourself, to wallow in guilt. That is too easy. I'm asking for you to tarry, to linger, with the ways in which you perpetuate a racist society, the ways in which you are racist. I'm now daring you to face a racist history which, paraphrasing Baldwin, has placed you where you are and that has formed your own racism. Again, in the spirit of Baldwin, I am asking you to enter into battle with your white self. I'm asking that you open yourself up; to speak to, to admit to, the racist poison that is inside of you.

Again, take a deep breath. Don't tell me about how many Black friends you have. Don't tell me that you are married to someone of color. Don't tell me that you voted for Obama. Don't tell me that *I'm* the racist. Don't tell me that you don't see color. Don't tell me that I'm blaming whites for everything. To do so is to hide yet again. You may have never used the N-word in your life, you may hate the KKK, but that does not mean that you don't harbor racism and benefit from racism. After all, you are part of a system that allows you to walk into stores where you are not followed, where you get to go for a bank loan and your skin does not count against you, where you don't need to engage in "the talk" that Black people and people of color must tell their children when they are confronted by white police officers.

As you reap comfort from being white, we suffer for being Black and people of color. But your comfort is linked to our pain and suffering. Just as my comfort in being male is linked to the suffering of women, which makes me sexist, so, too, you are racist. That is the gift that I want you to accept, to embrace. It is a form of knowledge that is taboo. Imagine the impact that the acceptance of this gift might have on you and the world.

Take another deep breath. I know that there are those who will write to me in the comment section with boiling anger, sarcasm, disbelief, denial. There are those who will say, "Yancy is just an angry Black man." There are others who will say, "Why isn't Yancy telling Black people to be honest about the violence in their own Black neighborhoods?" Or "How can Yancy say that all white people are racists?" If you are saying these things, then you've already failed to listen. I come with a gift. You're already rejecting the gift that I have to offer. This letter is about *you*. Don't change the conversation. I assure you that so many Black people suffering from poverty and joblessness, which are linked to high levels of crime, are painfully aware of the existential toll that they have had to face because they are Black and, as Baldwin adds, *"for no other reason."*[3]

Some of your white brothers and sisters have made this leap. The legal scholar Stephanie M. Wildman, has written, "I simply believe that no matter how hard I work at not being racist, I still am. Because part of racism is systemic, I benefit from the privilege that I am struggling to see."[4] And the journalism professor Robert Jensen: "I like to think I have changed, even though I routinely trip over the lingering effects of that internalized racism and the institutional racism around me. Every time I walk into a store at the same time as a black man and the security guard follows him and leaves me alone to shop, I am benefiting from white privilege."[5]

What I'm asking is that you first accept the racism within yourself, accept all of the truth about what it means for you to be white in a society that was created for you. I'm asking for you to trace the binds that tie you to forms of domination that you would rather not see. When you walk into the world, you can walk with assurance; you have already signed a contract, so to speak, that guarantees you a certain form of social safety.

Baldwin argues for a form of love that is "a state of being, or state of grace—not in the infantile American sense of being made happy but in the tough and universal sense of quest and daring and growth."[6] Most of my days, I'm engaged in a personal and societal battle against sexism. So many times, I fail. And so many times, I'm complicit. But I refuse to hide behind that mirror that lies to me about my "non-sexist nobility." Baldwin says, "Love takes off the masks that we fear we cannot live without and know we cannot live within."[7] In my heart, I'm done with the mask of sexism, though I'm tempted every day to wear it. And, there are times when it still gets the better of me.

White America, are you prepared to be at war with yourself, your white identity, your white power, your white privilege? Are you prepared to show me a white self that love has unmasked? I'm asking for love in return for a gift; in fact, I'm hoping that this gift might help you to see yourself in ways that you have not seen before. Of course, the history of white supremacy in America belies this gesture of Black gift-giving, this gesture of non-sentimental love. Martin Luther King Jr. was murdered even as he loved.

Perhaps the language of this letter will encourage a split—not a split between Black and white, but a fissure in your understanding, a space for loving a Trayvon Martin, Eric Garner, Tamir Rice, Aiyana Stanley-Jones, Sandra Bland, Laquan McDonald, and others. I'm suggesting a form of love that enables you to see the role that you play (even despite your anti-racist actions) in a *system* that continues to value Black lives on the cheap.

Take one more deep breath. I have another gift.

If you have young children, before you fall off to sleep tonight, I want you to hold your child. Touch your child's face. Smell your child's hair. Count the fingers on your child's hand. See the miracle that is your child. And then, with as much vision as you can muster, I want you to imagine that your child is Black.

In peace,
George Yancy

DEAR NIGGER
PROFESSOR

If you are white, and you've made it through the first chapter, welcome to *your* world—a world where I am deemed a "nigger." But before you throw this book across the room declaring your "white innocence," and how guilty I am for making such inane generalizations, hang in there with me. I assure you that this is not a case of "reverse racism," especially as I've never had that kind of power. I did not ask for this world or its white racist sickness and violence directed toward me and other Black people and people of color, but here I am, and here *you* are. And I understand that you did not ask for it either, but our relationship to that world (*your world*) is fundamentally different. You see, in that world, you are treated as a human being and I am not; I'm deemed a nigger. And while you may never have used the term "nigger" as an insult, an utterance of dehumanization, you will need to understand that your whiteness, and how you live your whiteness, is vouchsafed at the expense of my being deemed a nigger. It is not always what you say that does the harm; it is also what you don't say, what you fail to say, refuse to say. Your silence and indifference have implications for my life—Black life. The harm that you also perpetuate, and this point will require more understanding and a great deal of openness on your part, results from how you, as a white person, are positioned structurally within this world of "ours." I will say more about this later in the book, but understand that while that may be hard for you to understand and even harder for you to admit and take responsibility for, it is far more difficult (deadly even) for me when you fail to understand, refuse to admit, and reject any responsibility. Lastly, I ask that you *not* treat the vile and racist disclosures in this chapter as aberrations. This is not a peep show, a private viewing of racist hatred and desires of a few white racist "deviants." This is about white America, not exceptions to it, but dimensions of its oppressive rule, its deep historic racist white imaginary, and its normative structure.

I take the title of this chapter from the beginning of a message that was sent to me after the publication of Dear White America, the letter that begins this book. It is a "salutation" designed to put me in "my place" or to remind me of "my place." It is designed to dehumanize, to degrade, perhaps to kill me softly. "Dear," preceding "nigger," is like saying "My beloved piece of shit." There is nothing to be cherished here despite the greeting. Malcolm X had this figured out years ago. He asks, "What does a white man call a Black man with a PhD?" The answer, according to Malcolm X, is "A Nigger with a PhD."[1] Had I been born Irish under certain historical circumstances, I would have been called a "white nigger," but at least they had the opportunity to drop the term nigger and "become white." In other words, for the Irish, the term nigger was probationary, borrowed only to modify the Irish until they proved otherwise—that is, "worthy" of whiteness. The idea that nigger can be used as a qualifying epithet for non-Black groups of people only proves its particular damaging intent.[2] In this sense, the term nigger is, as Randall Kennedy writes, "the paradigmatic slur."[3] He argues, "It is the epithet that generates epithets. That is why Arabs are called sand niggers, Irish the niggers of Europe, and Palestinians the niggers of the Middle East."[4]

Joe Feagin provides a deeper framework for understanding Kennedy's claim about the term nigger being the paradigmatic slur. While Feagin understands the historical and current ways in which people of color (including Chinese, Japanese, and Mexicans) have been "defined by many whites as somehow sub-human, noncitizens without rights, or second-class citizens,"[5] he understands how social mobility has functioned more positively vis-à-vis many non-Black people. Hence, Feagin writes, "White-on-black racism is thus a—if not *the*—crucial paradigmatic case of racism historically and in the present."[6] Much earlier, Fanon noted, "In Europe, that is to say, in every civilized and civilizing country, the Negro [nigger] is the symbol of sin. The archetype of the lowest values is represented by the Negro."[7]

It appears, then, that within the white imaginary, no matter how much "progress," no matter how much education, no matter how much wealth, no matter how much exercise of social respectability and class standing, or position of authority, say, president of the United States, no matter how phenotypically light (once *any* Black ancestry is discovered according to the "one-drop" rule), *I am a nigger*. It is not, when applied to me, a probationary term. Indeed, although the concept of race emerged within the context of modernity, "the nigger" takes on a reality of its own, as if, in the minds of those using the term, predating modernity. It *appears* then that to be a nigger is to be something "eternal," noncontingent. A nigger, in short, functions, within the white imaginary, as something metaphysical, not *socially* metaphysical, but applying to things "immutable"—*timeless*.

While Albert Memmi does not use the term nigger, he understands what is at stake temporally and metaphysically when discussing Black people within a context where "racial differences," predicated upon white racism, are deemed *final*.[8] He says, "there must be no loophole."[9] The process of totalization vis-à-vis the nigger "extends through time, back into the past and forward into the future."[10] According to white racism, "the Black man [woman] has always been inferior . . . the Black man [woman] will always be inferior."[11] There is a movement from biological myths regarding the Black body as repulsive (while paradoxically at other times sexually alluring) to its characterization as evil, to the removal of rights and political standing, to its status as metaphysically fixed. Within the context of white racism, Memmi states, "We go from biology to ethics, from ethics to politics, from politics to metaphysics."[12] As such, nigger appears to function as if it is a metaphysical category. It is *as if* being a nigger is an instantiation of a Platonic form—*The Nigger*.

I'm a "nigger professor" in virtue of being a nigger. As you read through this chapter, keep the following in mind. Who or what I am alleged to be is governed by a racist law of identity—"A nigger is a nigger." Frantz Fanon was on to this where he writes, *"Wherever he goes, the Negro* [the nigger] *remains a Negro* [a nigger]."[13]

After the publication of Dear White America, I received hundreds of combined emails, phone messages, and letters, in addition to the comments in the comments section at The Stone, *the New York Times*, in response to the article. While some of these were positive, and I will provide examples later in the book, there was an overwhelming number that were filled with white racist vitriol. I don't focus on the supportive responses in this chapter because my point is to expose what you may assume are just a small group of white individuals, an "aberration," who need to be educated. My aim is to tie these emails and phone calls into something much deeper and systemic that has a multitude of ways of hiding from the white view.[14]

Even white supremacist websites were immediately ablaze with white racist hatred regarding my letter. For me, visiting these websites was a little like snooping around within all white spaces undetected and being able to listen to what white people talk about in my absence. Many spoke to each other about me, a *white* call and response. I was the target of their hatred. The logic of their malicious claims spoke to the ways in which white people framed my existence and the existence of Black people according to a metaphysics of the nigger, the "fixedness" of what it means to be Black. I speak from the American context, which is the only context within which I have been unabashedly called a nigger; it is the place I call "home." And the following is what my white "family members" think of me.

"Another uppity Nigger. Calling a Nigger a professor is like calling White Black and Wet Dry."

"Even the most sophisticated nigger will revert back to their jungle bunny behavior when excited."

"You can dress a Nigger up in a suit and tie and they'll still be Niggers."

"This belief that niggers even reason is blatant pseudo-intellectualism."

As the first white writer makes clear, a "nigger professor" is an oxymoron, something pointedly foolish. And since I am allegedly a nigger, I damn sure cannot be a professor. Look, white can't be black, and wet can't be dry. Hence, as the racist logic goes, a nigger can't be a professor. And even if I have been academically groomed at an Ivy League (for me, Yale), I'm still a "jungle bunny" according to the next writer. And notice that I will revert, I will relapse back into my "primitive" and "criminal" state despite my extensive education. Just call me "Dr. Jungle Bunny." Joe Feagin writes, "The gendered racism that most whites also directed at black women routinely viewed them as having 'jungle bunny' sexual desires and procreative abilities."[15] Have I been rendered "effeminate" or have Black women been "masculinized"? Within the white imaginary both processes can serve racist aims. For example, if Black men are effeminized or emasculated, they cannot pose a sexual threat to white men. If Black women are masculinized, then they are not deserving of protection—they have no delicate "feminine sensibilities" to shelter.[16] Nevertheless, what emerges is a case where what I am does not allow for exceptions. Remember: A nigger is a nigger. After all, as the third writer says, I can be decked out in my finest and I will still be a nigger. There is no escape. Clothes will not conceal the "real" me. The fourth person claims that I can't genuinely engage in reasoning. And this person probably has not read the racist views of Kant,[17] Hegel,[18] or Jefferson,[19] who each made similar claims about Black people being bereft of the capacity to reason. This entire book that you're holding must be a farce. Perhaps I'm just parroting (like philosopher Hume[20] would say of Black people) what I've already heard. I'm just a nigger who dared to reason only to discover that reason is white. I pretend to reason; a pseudo-process.

"[The] Nigger in the white house is a usurper of the office not a bona fide president."

"The concept of there being an intellectual Negro is a joke."

"Dear nigger . . . fuck you, I am racist, I'm ok with that now thanks to your nigger community and their actions over the last few years."

"STFU [shut the fuck up], and be thankful for your birth in America, because tomorrow morning when you wake up you'll STILL just be another whining, begging, gimme-dat, nigger. But here you are at least by law a protected and coddled 2nd class citizen. Anywhere else, you would be dead . . ."

Obama, according to the first writer in this group of quotes, being the nigger that he apparently is, was never really qualified to be president. And apparently not duly elected, indeed, not even born an American citizen, he just seized control of the White House. We can thank now President Trump for sustaining that malicious and nasty "birther" lie. Of course, Obama taught constitutional law at the University of Chicago Law School and was the first African American president of the *Harvard Law Review*, but I guess for the next writer that was a joke. The next writer at least calls me "Dear nigger." But wait, "fuck you" follows it. He/she gives me the middle finger. At least this writer is honest about him/herself: "I am a racist." Why? Well, because of Black people like me, the ones who all look alike and are alike. Apparently, our "nigger ways" wore away any decency that he/she had. Our "nigger actions" and our "nigger community" are to blame for this writer's racism. The writer also adds a sarcastic "thanks." So, let me get this right, if we were not niggers, he/she would not have been a racist? Strange. The last writer in the list would rather I not speak at all, and certainly not dare to write a letter called Dear White America. "Shut the fuck up," I'm told. Well, I guess that I should. After all, my PhD means nothing. And my reasoning capacity, well, that's just nonexistent. This person must have spoken to the white woman who left the following message on my university answering machine:

> Dear professor, I am a white American citizen. You are the one who is the racist against white people, evidently. A professor—I bet you got it [your PhD] through a mail order.

Notice how she speaks with authority, how her race, nationality, and legal standing are stated up front to carry weight, to attempt to silence me. And regarding my degree, well, I just picked up the phone, placed the order, and lo and behold my PhD appeared in the mail. And having procured my PhD in this way, as a nigger, wait, "a coon," it serves me well.

On one white racist website, one writer apparently has seen behind my entire game:

> This coon is a philosopher in the same way Martin King was a PHD and the same way that Jesse Jackson and Al Sharpton are 'Reverends': Just another jive assed nigger with a new way to pimp.

My last writer in the second group of four above, though, not only wants me to "Shut the fuck up," but to be thankful to have been born in America. No thanks! I'll be thankful when America undergoes a rebirth, something truly and robustly democratic, perhaps even a beloved community,[21] and not something politically and ethically stillborn. Yet even as I am told that I should be thankful to have been born in America, at the end of the day,

I'm still just a nigger in America because, as he/she says, "tomorrow morning when you wake up you'll STILL just be another whining, begging, gimme-dat, nigger." This writer also thinks, though, that I'm a second-class citizen. Many people in America are treated as second-class citizens, but not all second-class citizens are treated as niggers. Which is it in this writer's view? And apparently, I am by law "protected" and "coddled." Ask Trayvon Martin, Sandra Bland, Walter Scott, Philando Castile, Aiyana Stanley-Jones, and so many other Black people and people of color how it felt to be "protected" and "coddled." The writer adds, "Anywhere else, you would be dead." Is the writer saying that I should be happy to be in America because America keeps its Black citizens alive? Well, that is just a blatant lie. Or is the writer making a threat? Because I am a nigger, a whining, begging one at that, he/she would kill me (and other niggers) were it not for the fact that America "protects" us? We would be dead, because anywhere else we would not be tolerated? Or if it were not for laws that allegedly protect us, it would mean our immediate death, because we are niggers? This sounds genocidal to me.

I have never been called a nigger so many times in my life. And the number of times squeezed into such a short period of time felt like being called a nigger every hour of each day. You would think, then, that having been called a nigger so many times by white people who read my letter, Dear White America, as you will continue to read in the following pages, it would be easy to write this chapter, a chapter written *for you*—white America—*about you*. (Again, don't throw the book.) However, when I sat down to write this chapter, I experienced what felt like writer's block. I wondered whether it was because I was too close to the material. Yet this "block" was something that I couldn't afford to endure. Too much is at stake.

Surely my justified anger should have functioned as a catalyst for driving my fingers to hammer away at my keyboard, cathartically releasing all of the anxiety and outrage felt as a result of having the vile word nigger vomited in my face so many times. A spewing of foul-smelling hatred, lies, and distortions. But why waste time writing to white people about themselves? Why give you, white America, any more attention? After all, it has always been about you, about your place at the center. And even if you have veered from the center economically, you have never occupied the outer limits of being a "nigger."

Some of my students of color have said to me: "Why talk about race with white people when at the end of the day everything remains the same—that is, their racism continues?" "Why teach courses on race and whiteness?" "Do you really think that such courses will make a difference?" "You must know that white people just don't give a damn." Personally, I find these questions haunting; they frequent my conscience.

Indeed, there are times when I ask myself, "Why do I do this?" After all, I don't write about whiteness because it is a new fad in philosophy. I don't have the privilege. And I'm certainly not a masochist. There is no pleasure to be had in being the object of white hatred, violence, and sexually perverse white desires to mutilate the Black body, which historically white people have done. Even their white children came to the "barbeque" (white people's term, not mine). I'm sure that a few of my Black colleagues and colleagues of color think that I've lost my sanity. Perhaps they think that I've asked for all of this and that had I remained silent I would have been fine. The reality, of course, is that, at the end of the day, they too are seen as niggers. Silence will not help. Hell, perhaps even a few "enlightened" white folk think that what I'm doing is fruitless. Perhaps when alone even they have their doubts, silently admitting to themselves that they are not ready to face their whiteness with the kind of honesty that is required.

Keep in mind that in Dear White America I asked white people to listen with love. I was asking for a form of love, though, that demands the removal of masks, a love that wrenches the soul. I referred to the letter as a gift, albeit a heavy one. It seems strange to offer a gift when white people have already taken everything. Indeed, what is there to give? I don't know, perhaps the truth about themselves. Moreover, there is an inner voice that continues to haunt me: "Why give white folk anything? *They* don't deserve anything that you have to offer." Also, given their history and vile treatment of Black bodies, how can you ask for *love* in return for the *gift* of the letter? I ask all of this knowing that we as Black people should not (*must not*) play the role of "superhuman" moral actors in the face of white violence within a country that continues to find ways of niggerizing us. I recall one Black woman calling me out during a Q&A after a talk that I gave on whiteness and the Black body: "How can you ask that we give white people a gift, be their 'saviors,' and yet continue to function as the recipients of their hatred?" While I never said anything about being their "saviors," this was yet another question that has come to haunt me.

The facts speak for themselves. As shown previously, the gift was returned by countless readers and draped in the form of that ugly, vile word—*nigger*. In fact, on one website a white contributor wrote the following in response to my letter, the one for which I asked for love in return. It was kind of like LeBron James's experience when the word nigger was spray-painted on the front gate of his multimillion dollar home.[22] I say, "kind of like" because of the sheer number of iterations directed at me:

nigger, nigger.

When alone (and this is meant for anyone to do), try reading the iterations of the word nigger full-throated, aloud and slow, and perhaps it might begin, as it does for me, to trigger not just anger, but profound grief and sorrow. For me, speaking each instance aloud, emphasizing each discrete syllable, making sure to articulate it with clarity, touches a space often hidden in my soul. I begin to feel the precious reality of my own humanness, the humanness of my mother, my children. And I can't take it anymore. It's as if something—a scream, a cry—is trying to get out of my throat, lodged somewhere deeper in my chest. But I close the exit. I have felt this articulation with even greater intensity when reading the word over and over again before a large audience. But I refuse to show white people a tear. Anger is better!

Essentially, that was the response of one reader, a series of the word "nigger," "nigger," "nigger," "nigger," "nigger," running down the entire screen. It was clear what the white reader thought of me. The white reader didn't critically engage the letter. It was not, as we say in philosophy, read charitably. Then again, perhaps the reader was generous or charitable in his/her honest response. This could have been his/her way of "saving" me from all of my "delusions" about being anything but a "nigger"; perhaps a kind of profoundly disturbing and perverse "charity." The reader decided to write what he/she thinks is true and so told it like it is—"You're a nigger!" Then again, perhaps he/she spared me a greater fate through the use of a racial epithet rather than through the all too well-known actions of a white racist American pastime: the brutalization of Black bodies, vicious beatings and killings, and the hanging of strange fruit—Black bodies swinging in the trees with broken necks and mutilated bodies.

"Oh, but surely, Yancy, you exaggerate." *No, on the contrary, I understate*. White crimes against Black bodies have yet to be told in full. The discourse to do so will be forged from a collective Black *affective* capacity that continues to intensify due to layer after layer, trauma after trauma, of white terror, white arrogance, white inhumanity, violence by white police and their proxies, white microaggressions and macroaggressions, dehumanizing white gazes, dismissive white gestures, and, lest I forget or pretend as though it does not exist—the harsh racism from my white "allies." You know, the ones who say that they've got my back, that they understand the nuance and complexity of my scholarship, that they respect my epistemological integrity, that they refuse to use me *as experience* for their own *theoretical ends*, that they despise the use of the N-word, and that they really do *see me for who and what I am*. Really?

In 2015, I was invited to be a plenary speaker at a well-established philosophy conference where the topic of the body was taken seriously within the framework of a phenomenological perspective.[23] I was excited. After all, I was there to deliver my talk within the company of kindred philosophical spirits, those who knew something about feminism, disability, aesthetics, and race, and how these areas address important questions regarding the body or embodiment. Besides me, there was one other Black philosopher in attendance, though he was older, taller in height, very gray and heavier; all of the other philosophers and attendees were white. The day after I gave my talk, the other Black philosopher shared with me that several conference attendees had approached him with no apparent hesitancy or ambiguity. "That was a *very* important talk that you gave yesterday," one white philosopher said to him. Another white philosopher said, "Wow, great talk!" "Inspiring," came from another. No less than seven congratulatory gestures were made. Had there been one, perhaps it could have been brushed off as an honest mistake. Even after the second time, though feeling a bit uneasy, one might even have been able to excuse it. However, this was not a *faux pas*, a false step. Seven times? Are you serious? This was the manifestation of an all-too-familiar mode of being white— white habits of perception, white racist iterative processes of seeing Black people as all the same through a fixed *imago*. This was about white racism. My colleague, the Black philosopher who had *not* given the talk, somehow "became" me and I, him.

Within that rich, sophisticated, philosophically progressive white space, I could hear a strange and profoundly irritating echo of the little white child who Frantz Fanon encountered on a train: "Look, a Negro!"[24] There was a familiar sense of being fixed, static. Fanon says, "A man was expected to behave like a man. I was expected to behave like a black man—or at least like a nigger."[25] In retrospect, I wonder *what* they had heard, *who* they had heard deliver the plenary. The two of us became *one* Black man; *any* Black man; *every* Black man; perhaps *any* nigger. Keep in mind that this space was supposed to be "safe." Yet given this experience, it was hostile, belittling, violent, and dehumanizing. And this from my white allies? We were flattened out, seen as surface things, one-dimensional, indistinct and repeatable. We were excessive; one Black identifiable mass. The whites failed to see *me*, and they failed to see *him*. It was not that I was stopped and frisked by New York's finest. Yet there was that same sense of being profiled, placed under a racial typology that allowed for no nuance. Both are experiences of a form of confiscation, where the meaning of my Black body is seized by white gazes. As Fanon writes, "I am fixed. Having adjusted their microtomes, they objectively cut away slices of my reality. I am laid bare."[26]

Within a different historical context, I would have been lynched because some white woman said that a Black man had accosted and raped her, though I was nowhere close to the alleged act. Lynching *any* Black male body that "fit the description" would have been sufficient; indeed, within the context of American white supremacy, the brutalization of any Black body would have served the larger purpose of white nation building, of protecting the "purity" and "innocence" of whiteness, especially white women. And if a Black woman protested such unjust brutality, the "nigger bitch" would have no doubt first been brutally raped, or perhaps burned alive while pregnant and her unborn baby cut from her abdomen, only to have its little, fragile skull crushed beneath some white man's boot heel after it fell and hit the ground. This was the tragic reality of twenty-one-year-old Mary Turner in Lowndes County, Georgia, in 1918.[27]

I don't think that I could remain intact if I attempted to hold alive in my spirit all the absurd and cruel contradictions experienced by Black people in America under white supremacy, the spoken and unspoken terror and violence visited upon them. I would surely be torn asunder, belying the "dogged strength" that W. E. B. Du Bois claimed of Black people.

As you continue to read this chapter, I want to remind you again of the love I requested in return for the gift of my letter. Imagine a gift that is offered, a gift wrapped in vulnerability, a gift that is precarious, a term whose root meaning involves a process of asking, an entreaty, a prayer.[28] That describes my letter to white America, a letter that asks white people to address, as best they can, their own racism and the systemic nature of that racism. Now, imagine the sound, the fury, the rage of white people spewing ugly and racist words designed to threaten, to dehumanize, to hurt, to intimidate me.

It is the manifestation of this rage that I heard as I listened to the messages recorded on my university answering machine. The following recorded messages are part of the price to be paid for reaching out, in love, to white America to face its racism. When I think about these recorded messages, I become infuriated by any talk of a postracial America. These recordings belie the truth of any such claim. White America fails to be daring when it comes to facing the historical legacy and contemporary manifestations of its racism. The centuries of existential struggle faced by Black people is mocked by white America's long-standing desire and seemingly unbreakable will to continue to attempt to truncate Black people in the form of a nigger. Because of our collective dehumanized treatment within the belly of the American beast, so many of America's ideals ring hollow to us. This is why James Baldwin writes, "White people cannot, in the generality, be taken as models of how to live."[29] The following four recordings, repulsive beyond words, speak to Baldwin's contention.

Dear Nigger Professor. You are a fucking racist. You are a piece of shit destroying the youth of this country. You are neither African nor American. You are pure, 100 percent Nigger. You would never marry outside of your Nigger race. That's a fact. You're a fucking smug Nigger. You are uneducated with education. You are a fucking animal. Just like all Black people in the United States of America. Including that Nigger Kenyan that was born in fucking Kenya that has usurped the white house. Yes. It is called the white house for a reason because white people made this country great you fucking Nigger.

Where does one begin? Well, why not with the deep contradiction. This caller identifies me as "Nigger Professor" and *I am* somehow the "fucking racist"? I'm called a nigger, one of the nastiest words to exist, and yet somehow I magically become a racist for asking him to engage honestly his white racism. In my letter to white people, I never used such derogatory terms as "cracker," "redneck," "honky," "Miss Anne," "white trash," or "hillbilly." And even if I had used such terms, the gravity of the historical sting of the term nigger outweighs any nasty epithet used against white people. To argue otherwise is to be guilty of assuming a false equivalence. There is just no term used to degrade white people that depicts them as subhuman, and that was historically and is contemporarily used within a larger racist system designed to oppress white people.

This caller also calls me a "piece of shit." He has externalized me. I am the embodiment of disgust, that which is expelled from the body (the physical body and the white body politic) and must remain external to the purity of whiteness—that is, whiteness as a site of "cleanliness" or "virtue." As a "piece of shit," it is not even clear that I qualify as a "sub-person." As a "piece of shit," I will never make it to the obituary section.[30] As Joel Kovel writes, "In the white racist order, the Other is not a person at all."[31] And speaking directly to the racial implications of being called a "piece of shit," Kovel writes, "The fantasy of dirt and purification is the central theme of white racism from a subjective standpoint."[32] Perhaps this is why on another white racist website, in addition to being called a "silverback" and a "moolie," I was labeled "shitskin."

And similar to the accusations raised against Socrates vis-à-vis the Athenian youth, this caller accuses me of "destroying the youth of this country." Notice, too, that I am neither African nor American. I defy those categories. This would imply that some people are at least one or the other, but not me.

Furthermore, recall what I said earlier about metaphysics and the nigger being "immutable." The caller says that I am "pure, 100 percent Nigger."

According to white racist mythology, however, even if I had a mere drop of "Black blood," I would still be considered a nigger in white America. His use of "pure, 100 percent Nigger" sounds like a new species; it is one that is unalloyed, a teratological *thing* of polygenetic origins.

Notice that he also says that I *would never* marry outside my nigger race, not that I *could* never. I can, but I won't? Does "would never" imply that as a nigger I see white potential partners as undesirable? Or is it that I see them as desirable, but would decide against marrying them?

And notice that I'm an *arrogant* nigger—a "smug nigger." That must be the worst kind of nigger. I guess that a "humble nigger" is better. Still a nigger, though a preferred one.

He then says, "You are a fucking animal." It is true, of course, that all human beings are animals, not plants. He doesn't mean this, though, as a truism. I don't recall ever hearing someone refer to an elephant as a "*fucking* animal." I wonder what animal rights advocates would say about this situation. Clearly, he does not mean this as a compliment—to me or to animals! There is something about being a "fucking animal" that seems to be morally significant. And notice the use of *all*. There are no exceptions. Of course, I can't be certain about who he includes under the category of Black people, but I will assume that he means people like me, African American people (of course, I am not including white South Africans who happen to be in America). So, we are *all* "fucking animals." He also includes Obama, though he is referred to as a "Nigger Kenyan" who has, as we've seen earlier, managed to usurp the white house. Only this time, we are told that the White House is white because white people made this country "great." He ends by calling me a "Fucking Nigger"—lest I forget, I suppose.

Hey Georgie boy. You're the fucking racist, asshole. You wouldn't have a job if it wasn't for affirmative action. Somebody needs to put a boot up your ass and knock your fucking head off your shoulders you stupid fucking goddamn racist son of a bitch. You fucking race baiting son of a bitches. Man, you're just asking to get your fucking asses kicked. You need your fucking asses kicked. You stupid motherfucker. Quit fucking race baiting, asshole.

In this next phone message, I am "affectionately" called "Georgie boy." I am reminded that I would not have my job were it not for affirmative action. Yes. This is probably true. In fact, so many white women wouldn't have jobs either! This is an ironic claim given that white male affirmative action has been so effective over so many years. As a reminder, though, affirmative action is not white supremacy in reverse; it is not antiwhite, but pro-justice. It was created so that with my PhD, which I earned with distinction, I would actually be able to teach at a university. Just for the record, affirmative action, in the case of Black people, was created as a response to so many forms of prejudicial and systemic racist disadvantages against us. It's important to get that history right—not twisted.

The caller then follows this with an expressed desire for white physical violence. Indeed, for the love that I asked for in return, I'm told that "Somebody needs to put a boot up your ass and knock your fucking head off your shoulders." I'll slightly change the words of my first caller. Hey, that is "pure, 100 percent white violence." There is no getting around that one.

Notice, too, that I'm a "race baiter." Although I anticipated some form of white anger as a response to Dear White America, and even tried to address it in the letter, I did not intend to intimidate. And I did not anticipate the abhorrent degree of the white racist anger in response. My advanced response was that if you felt this particular emotion, you were missing my point, you were missing the gift. Look, I didn't create the problem of race/racism in America. White people are responsible for that. However, if "race baiting" is refusing to remain silent about white racism in America, then I must be guilty.

The white racist vulgarity continues. I'm also a "stupid fucking goddamn racist son of a bitch." That's a mouth full. I make no sense, I should be cursed (after all, he says, "goddamn"), I am a racist, and I was given birth to by a "bitch." It is here that I begin to feel that precious reality of the humanness of my Black mother that I mentioned earlier.

> You should go fuck yourself. Ok. Just go fuck yourself. You're [the] racist fucking prick here. You are exactly the problem. So, why don't you and Al Sharpton and Jessie-jackoffson all get together and circle jerk and shoot your fucking nut on each other's racist faces. You got the NAACP, you've got the Black Congressional Caucus, you've got BET television. You've got every fucking thing. I don't owe you a mother fucking thing, asshole. Not a fucking thing. So, why don't you go fuck yourself. Ok. You are fucking racist, you dick.

From this caller, I am told several times to "fuck yourself." After the second time, I'm also called a "prick." After those comments, he says, "You are exactly the problem." Strange. And then I am told to get together with two Black political figures and "circle jerk and shoot your fucking nut on each other's racist faces." So, I'm a racist. Al Sharpton is a racist. And Jessie Jackson is a racist. The reader should note that the sexual references are not just despicable white racist comments, but created from the white imaginary that is obsessed with Black male bodies. Are these meant as insults or intended as desired pleasures, things to behold? This is his white racist pornographic fantasy. Sorry, but I have no desire to be part of his white fantasy.

Note, too, that not only am I called a prick, but at the end I'm called a "dick." After all, within the white imaginary, as Fanon notes, "The Negro is the genital."[33] The sexually graphic nature of the caller's descriptions speak to white fantasies of, in this case, Black male hypersexuality. This raises important questions about sex and race. The intersection of sex and race is a twisted and perverse staple within the white imaginary. Cornel West writes, "White fear of black sexuality is a basic ingredient of white racism."[34] Of course, this "fear" is inextricably linked to white desire and sexual fantasies. Fanon writes, "A [white] prostitute told me that in her early days the mere thought of going to bed with a Negro brought on an orgasm."[35] We also know that white men would rape Black women and blame it on the irresistible "hypersexuality" of the Black women themselves. According to this racist logic, a Black woman can't be raped if she always desires sex.

The hypersexualization of the Black body is a theme that I encountered many times on white supremacist websites directed at me. As you read them, keep saying to yourself that this is not a dream. This is twenty-first-century white America during Obama's presidency, our first African American president. Don't believe the hype about a postracial America. In so many ways, white America is still what it used to be.

This ugly fucking nigger is just asking for access to more white females.

I wrote Dear White America, a letter that asks white people to examine their racism, to have access to more white females? And given that I'm supposedly an "ugly fucking nigger," I guess that this was my deceptive ploy. Otherwise, how could I have pulled it off? My objective, according to this white racist madness, is to talk to white people about their racism, and white women will flock to me. White America, what is crucial about this is that this white person actually believes this.

Furthermore, I guess that I cannot be a "handsome nigger"; there is obviously something mutually exclusive there. So, I'm called an "ugly nigger." Well, actually, "fucking" is interpolated between "ugly" and "nigger." Look, the writer of this comment did not engage the letter, certainly not critically. All that he can see is that the letter functions as access to more white females. What does this say about *this* white person? More broadly, what does this say about the racially distorted perceptual and interpretive frames of reference embedded within white American culture that mediate how white people make sense of Black intentions? It is the likes of such racist mediations that can and do lead to the death of unarmed Black people by white police officers.[36]

> The thing is these blacks are not dumb they know they are manipulating white idiots, especially white women into literally sucking their dicks.

So, again, though more graphic, Dear White America was written as a way of deceiving white people. In this case, at least I'm not dumb. Really, though? After reading Dear White America, white women will be lining up to perform oral sex on me? This is both an insult to me and to white women. Yet it speaks to something sickening about white distortions of reality. As a Black man, if I write a letter, a research paper, hell, why not a book, white women will be eager to perform fellatio on me. Whose desire is this really? What does the writer desire to see? If there was ever a case of projection, this is it.

> This man's sickness is not that uncommon, and it is tempting to some. Some women, and some men, will want to sleep with him, mistaking his siren song for love.

This time, with such audacity, I'm said to be sick. However, it is not that uncommon. It is apparently more widespread. It must be one of those exotic sicknesses, like *Drapetomania*, which was said to make Black people run away from plantations, or *Dysaesthesia aethiopica*, which was said to make Black people, among other things, break tools. According to this writer, the sickness appears to be my uncontrollable, maniacal cunning to deceive at least some white people, men and women, into getting them to sleep with me. It is a sickness that has the power to seduce. In this case, more specifically, my sickness compels me to write a letter that is really tough on white people, and some white people will be so seduced by what I have to say to them that they will *want* to sleep with me after reading the letter. The love that I asked for in return for the gift is really a hidden strategy, dictated by my "sickness," to seduce white people.

According to the writer, I'm also a Black mythical creature, a Siren, luring white people into my bed and therefore to their doom. Keep in mind that this is the stuff of white sexual perversion and distortion. It is this white madness and violence that was unleashed on Black men and boys who were said to have desired a white woman, or "raped" a white woman, or to have looked at or even startled a white woman. Dear White America must have touched the very souls of white people, unleashing, among other things, historically deadly forms of white sexual fantasies projected onto the Black male body, *my body*. Keep in mind, twenty-one-year-old white male Dylan Roof shot and killed nine African Americans as they attended a Bible study at the historic Emanuel AME Church in Charleston, South Carolina. One reason that he gave for the massacre is that, "Y'all are raping our white women."

If you are white reading this, what do you make of those three responses? Given the history of white America's obsession with Black sexuality, these responses are not aberrations; they speak to deep forms of white cultural consciousness, forms of white insularity, white nativism, and white nation building. For the record, Europe was also sexually obsessed with Black bodies. Could it be a *global* white projection?

Returning to the third phone message, the ridiculously exaggerative part of the message is that after the caller names three Black sites of empowerment (NAACP, the Black Congressional Caucus, and BET), he says that Black people have *everything*. This is clearly white hyperbole and overestimation.[37] I assume that the caller has never heard about the ways in which white America has, because of white privilege and white power, always advanced white people, or that Congress is predominantly white, or heard of WET (white entertainment television), almost every TV channel other than BET.

This caller reminds me and other Black people that he does not owe us "a mother fucking thing." In Dear White America, I asked for honesty, acknowledgment of one's white racism, its collective and systemic reality, and love in return for a gift. Perhaps the caller thought that somewhere within my letter I was asking for reparations. An ethically repaired white world will require more than that.

You dumb ass living piece of shit.

This last caller also identifies me as feces, but makes sure to comment on my lack of intelligence and the fact that I'm not just any piece of shit, but, as he says, "You dumb ass living piece of shit." By adding "living," I'm transmogrified into something like a walking, talking, breathing piece of shit, perhaps a nuanced biological category altogether. On one white racist website, a message from someone who thought that I no longer deserved to keep my job, was written, "You should be fired now, you sick, racist POS [Piece Of Shit]." Fanon notes that "The Negro symbolizes the biological."[38] Does this mean that I symbolize all of the excretions from the body—excrement, urine, semen, blood, phlegm, pus? If so, I appear to be associated with all of those things that, for the most part, force us to recoil.

Reading white racist vitriol written by white people can be traumatic. In fact, I felt sickened reading one letter, out of quite a few, sent to me through regular postal mail, which was handwritten and signed. There was something even more sickening than reading an email message or a post on a website given the level of industry expended to write it, put it in an envelope, address it and put a stamp on it, and mail it off. The opening of the letter read, "*I'm* a racist? How *dare* you call me that! *You* are a racist and, hey, since blacks call each other 'nigga' I'm taking the liberty of doing the same. Either the word is offensive and taboo or it isn't."

Sorry, but I'm not buying it. For me, "nigga" remains off limits to you— *white folk*. You know, as ridiculous as it may sound, I once had two white male students in one of my classes attempt to make the case that they should be allowed to use the word nigger (with the "er") pretty much willy-nilly and that it is discriminatory to say that they can't. I must say that there are times when whiteness can suck the oxygen right out of the air. Any response at all felt too generous. I have often witnessed white people express the feeling of being somehow left out, especially within contexts where

Black people have found it necessary to carve out spaces for themselves, spaces that don't exclude white people because of so-called Black racism, but spaces that are necessary for Black sanity precisely because of white racism. It is as if white people are obsessed with a colonial desire to possess everything. Du Bois writes, "I do not laugh. I am quite straight-faced as I ask soberly: 'But what on earth is whiteness that one should so desire it?' "[39] To which he answers, "Then always, somehow, some way, silently but clearly, I am given to understand that whiteness is the ownership of the earth forever and ever, Amen!"[40] These two white students spoke with arrogance and the desire for total white ownership, to say whatever they felt like saying despite the white violence and ugliness associated with the word nigger. It was not so much that these two white students were deprived of historical knowledge; rather, that this knowledge meant little or nothing when it came to their sense of "loss of power."

Anyway, the letter writer proceeds, "Niggas are largely uncivilized savages who have been ruined by food stamps, welfare, [and] affirmative action." He concludes, "Well, George, since you say I'm a racist, I'd better start being one." This line reminded me of another white male student who said, "Because you say that I'm a racist, I might as well be the best racist that I can be." Following this ridiculous logic, because men are rightly critiqued for being sexists, then we ought to find new ways of degrading women and ourselves. He completely missed the point. Being a white racist, what I call in some cases an antiracist racist, can and must be fought against. More on this later in the book.

The letter writer concluded, "Write some more letters, nigga. Put on yo' ball cap and look smug. Go to hell, jerkfuck." Well, it is true that I wear a ball cap. There is that word smug again. After all, it's just a photo. By the way, I have no desire to go to hell. And a "jerkfuck"? Well, your guess is as good as mine. But whatever it is, I'm supposedly it.

As I said, to read white racist vitriol can be traumatic. To *hear* white racist vitriol, however, can intensify the impact. Audibly, one gets to hear the inflection of the voice, its loudness, its nervousness filled with so much hate, its terror. When I wrote Dear White America, I had not anticipated the impact of the responses, written and spoken. I didn't know the extent to which the words would traumatize, that the words would wound. My physiology registered the wounds. Mood swings. Irritability. Trepidation. Disgust. Anger. Nausea. Words do things; they carry the vestiges of the bloody and brutal contexts within which they were animated. One might think that being called a nigger so many times might decrease its impact, blunted by anticipation. Given its history—*not at all*. The wound deepens; predominantly white spaces force a second look over your shoulder, not because of unfounded racist prejudices, but because of the facts of white American history. All of these damned calls, letters, email messages, racist website posts, actually substantiated what I had wanted to approach with the risk and daring of mutual vulnerability—*the realities of white racism*. These were forms of white racism concretized through a litany of ugly words, nasty terms, and filthy accusations. I could feel the sickness of bloodlust.

Nigger, as a racist epithet, in the mouths of white people, is inseparable from the word's brutal, bloody, and violent history. It was the weight of that history that was communicated in those threatening messages from white people. Nigger! Nigger! Nigger! There is white twisted pleasure gained when this word is shouted. Historically, to scream nigger was powerful enough to create a commotion that led to the mobilization of white bodies. Visualize the scene. White faces with looks of excitement and anger; a site of sexual perversity. A space filled with bloodlust and cruelty. Little white children brought to witness the spectacle; the so-called Black barbeque. In the air is the smell of burning Black flesh. The Black body torn to bits. "The nigger deserved it! After all, he had it coming." "Look, the rapist!" "There's the Coon!" "Black primitive!" One can see the Black body hanging from some tree; the Black body's neck broken; and, for some, their genitalia removed, fingers, toes, and ears cut off. One can see white people taking pictures, selling and buying parts of the nigger's brutalized body. *This is white terror.* "All black people in the United States, irrespective of their class status or politics," according to bell hooks, "live with the possibility that they will be terrorized by whiteness."[41]

The many responses of white people to Dear White America were just that—twenty-first-century white terror. That terror can come in many forms. Perhaps there is a Black man who finds it hard to breathe, even as he screams, "I can't breathe!" Perhaps he screams this call of help eleven times, but no one cares (Eric Garner[42]). Or perhaps after he has been shot by "accident," he musters enough strength to be outraged by it and then says aloud that he's losing his breath (Eric Harris[43]), only to hear a white police officer respond, "Fuck your breath!" Perhaps his spine gets severed

(Freddie Gray[44]). Perhaps he is a teenager and is shot sixteen times (Laquan McDonald[45]) as he walks away. Even reaching for and pulling out a wallet that "looks like a gun" can lead to getting shot at forty-one times and hit with nineteen bullets (Amadou Diallo[46]). According to white racist logic, these Black bodies are disposable. Then again, perhaps she is an innocent seven-year-old (Aiyana Stanley-Jones[47]) sleeping within the "safety" of her home, and yet killed by police during a raid. Just like for Emmett Till, there is no place that one can call safe in America for Black bodies. Perhaps playing the role of a secret agent (like white English actor Daniel Craig) is not a game meant for Black boys. Toy guns mysteriously become lethal in the hands of Black young boys (Tamir Rice[48]). Or, as a young Black woman, sitting at a segregated counter will result in white spit on her face, bruises to her head and back. White mobs screaming obscenities in her face. That is white terror. For whites, the nigger is unwanted; she is not good enough to inhabit the "civilized" monochromatic space of whiteness. Like knocking on a door for help (Renisha McBride[49]), her life can be taken because her Blackness is a "violation" of white space, white purity, white safety.

Du Bois, in a speech that he delivered in Peking, China, at the age of ninety-one, summed up an important message that all too familiarly speaks to Black life in America. He said, "In my own country for nearly a century I have been nothing but a nigger."[50] What if to be Black in white America is, in fact, to be nothing but a nigger? The historical record speaks for itself. Then, what does it mean to live life in a constant and unrelenting state of trauma? And what if, even during those snatched moments of respite, of feeling happy, joyous, one's life is, as Theo Shaw[51] powerfully said to me, like being on death row—just waiting to die? Sure, experience is open, time moves forward, history marches onward, but that openness does not necessarily arrest the reality of the pain of being categorized and treated like a nigger, a *thing* created from the white imaginary. I might extrapolate from the past: "Well, white racism isn't what it used to be." And yet, I'm still treated as a nigger, even as there has been important changes—adjustments. As an institutional structure with enduring white practices and white symbolic orders, whiteness seems to have the capacity to maintain its hegemony through change. It bends but doesn't break. It consumes but doesn't choke. Whiteness allows for resistance, but Black bodies remain the same, trapped within a serious symbolic and material order where, indeed, it feels like just waiting to die. Such a life is impacted by what Henry A. Giroux refers to as a culture of cruelty and a discourse of humiliation. The two concepts capture "the institutionalization and widespread adoption of a set of values, policies, and symbolic practices that legitimate forms of organized violence against human beings increasingly considered disposable, leading inexorably to unnecessary hardships, suffering, and despair."[52]

By recounting, in explicit language, the white backlash that I encountered after writing Dear White America, those violent and dehumanizing racist modes of address, I risk the potential to re-traumatize, to undergo those mood swings yet again. The retelling is imperative, though. For too long, I have had Black students say to me that they feel unsafe at PWIs (Predominantly White Institutions). I must believe them. This book confirms their reality. And while they may not have been called a nigger to their faces, such white spaces position them as inconsequential, deny their Blackness through superficial concerns for "diversity," and take their complaints as instances of *individual* problems adjusting to new spaces. At PWIs, there is an entire ethos of white curricula designed for white people, while Black people and people of color undergo forms of deep stress within those white spaces. I bear witness to Black pain and suffering because the deniers are out there. For we are told that what *we know* in our very bodies to be true isn't credible, which is a different kind of violence, the epistemic kind. I have certainly experienced this. In fact, after an interview with Brad Evans in which we explored the concept of violence within the context of the backlash that I received for writing Dear White America,[53] and in which I shared specific instances of white hatred directed toward me as a result, I encountered white deniers of my experiences, white naysayers.

One white racist website in particular went into full combat mode to deny my testimony.

"Yeah. I doubt it. So, I'm betting this is total bullshit. Nobody sent this nigger any 'hate mail.' [Others] should challenge him to produce it, and if he can't, sue him for defamation. Dumb-ass nigger."

"Dear Professor Baboon, You were NOT violated, injured or broken."

"I'll take 'Stories that never happened' for $500."

I lie. I'm a bullshitter. I'm lampooned. And notice the use of "Baboon." The term is jarring. It rips away my humanity. Yet through the white gaze, it bespeaks my identity as a nigger, a simian. The consistent though painful reality is that I also encountered similar animalistic references directed at me on other white racist websites.

"This ignorant monkey has no audience but other ignorant monkeys."

"Colored monkeys are like stalker chicks who just won't leave you alone."

"This monkey isn't talking to me. He doesn't even know I exist."

"As I see it, the only people whose racism is a problem is colored monkeys. They don't want to live without White people. They CAN'T live without White people."

"Dear Black America, 'Let go of your "black victimhood" and bring your-self to the point of admission that "you hoodrats and pavement apes are the ones destroying black lives and communities." And in closing, "don't blame Whitey!"

Joe Feagin writes, "Among the most egregious stereotypes and images common in the dominant racial frame today is the old view of Black Americans as being somehow linked to the animal kingdom, especially to apes and monkeys."[54] Feagin also writes, "Such views are not limited to white extremists. In recent research studies, moreover, social psychologists have found that the association in ordinary white minds between black Americans and apes remains strong and emotion-laden."[55]

How is it that within the twenty-first century, Black people continue to occupy and signify the domain of the primitive? What does this say about white people, whiteness? The future of the "nigger" is apparently ontologically foreclosed, permanently rendered beyond the domain of the human.

While Dear White America was published before Donald Trump's presidency, the white hatred, vitriol, nasty, and violent threats that I received are totally consistent with the unabashed white supremacist hatred that undergirds and follows from Trump's election, especially from his own white neofascism, bullying, and his divisive and racially charged, disgusting, and xenophobic rhetoric. It is not by accident that pictures of Trump were displayed on those websites where I was called a nigger. It was as if the pictures were used to endorse the epithet. I have no doubt that his presidency and his white nativism have encouraged hate and vile forms of othering. We have yet to witness the full arsenal of the hate of which he and many of his followers are capable. In fact, according to the Southern Poverty Law Center, there were 867 cases that were counted of "hateful harassment or intimidation in the United States in the 10 days after the November 8 election."[56] Indeed, just days after the election there were spray-painted signs that read, "Black Lives Don't Matter and Neither Does Your Vote," "#FuckNiggers, #FuckAllPorchMonkeys," "Heil Trump," and "Make America White Again." Furthermore, there were spray-painted swastikas on buildings, and American Islamophobia where women were threatened for wearing their hijabs.

With the election of Trump, what we are witnessing is Faustian in nature—millions of people, predominantly white, willing and prepared to sell their souls for their own apparent economic interests and their white nationalist identity (and the feeling of "loss" thereof) at the expense of the vulnerable. But what if there is a broader racist narrative that impacted their decision to vote for Trump? What if they were also just tired of being treated like "niggers"? Perhaps for many white people, their "sense of failure and exclusion from modern life produces a chronically diminished [white] narcissism. Through his [her] desperate identification with the authoritarian, past or present [Trump], he [she] hopes to regain that necessary [white] pride."[57]

Trump, the new "white savior figure," had already confirmed the loyalty of his base, saying that he could stand in the middle of 5th Avenue and shoot somebody and wouldn't lose voters. That is the signature of a narcissist, one who is reckless, who can do no wrong in his eyes or in the eyes of his followers. That kind of self-obsession places ethics and democracy in abeyance; it is quick to lose sight of the safety of the entire and collective demos (the people). One who puts at risk the collective demos can be described as an idiot. In his analysis, Eric Anthamatten traces the meaning of the term to idiocy, which comes from the root *idios*, or "one's own." Hence, "idiocy was the state of a private or self-centered person,"[58] the kind of person who sacrifices the integrity of the political whole. From "I'd like to punch him in his face,"[59] which Trump said about a protester, to his posting of a video to his Twitter account where he mimics throwing to the floor and violently punching someone who is depicted as CNN,[60] Trump, in many ways, is actually the unblocked and uncontrolled id of what is most despicable in the history of white racist America—its history of vicious violence and deep hypocrisy.

The threshold for this type of infantilism, shamelessness, and debauchery would be next to null if Trump was Black. We would see effigies of a Black body lynched on the White House lawn. Funny, though I'm finding it hard to laugh, how Trump, because he is a *white person*, escapes *racialized critique*. I have never heard such a critique from pundits. And even though it would be fallacious to do so, an *ad hominem* attack, white privilege protects him. When Trump, as president, engages in ethical and political grotesqueries, he is deemed "a different kind of president." Had Obama been guilty of a fraction of what Trump is guilty of, "nigger" would have become Obama's first name. Then, again, perhaps there is no low threshold to be reached to be called a nigger. Being Black is sufficient. Again, I refer back to what I said about metaphysics earlier and the racist law of identity—"A nigger is a nigger." And as a "nigger" one must be dealt with as only a nigger deserves.

Some might say that these responses I have received are indications of the fragility of white people. Robin DiAngelo has written insightfully about what she calls "white fragility." She argues that white fragility involves a response or state where merely "a minimum amount of racial stress becomes intolerable, triggering a range of defensive moves. These moves include the outward display of emotions such as anger, fear, and guilt, and behaviors such as argumentation, silence, and leaving the stress-inducing situation."[61] The responses that I received, however, speak to something more extreme than just reactionary or unreceptive responses. Rather than "white fragility," these responses are ones that speak to deep forms of white world-making, ways of thinking and feeling about Black people that exceed a specific challenge to whiteness or an effort to mark whiteness or an attempt to call out whiteness. These responses come from a fundamental racialized formation of hatred, a cesspool of white imaginings, a profound white disgust for the Black body that exceed the responses to what DiAngelo calls "triggers."

Following Trump's election, the following email message was sent to my university inbox on November 22, 2016:

I read your rant regarding white people, and I'm proud to inform you that I will never feel any guilt or shame for being white or who I am. FUCK YOU you race baiting piece of shit! You're just another nigger with a chip on his shoulder that's looking for excuses to justify his hatred, and guess what ass-hole NOBODY WHITE GIVES A FUCK WHAT YOU THINK. My only regret is that I didn't hear your bullshit in person so that I could call you a FUCKING NIGGER to your face you worthless bitch, and then kick your black ass until you were half dead. FUCK OFF BOY.

Keep in mind that Dear White America was published eleven months earlier. The writer congratulates himself by saying that he will "never feel any guilt." Yet in Dear White America, I made it clear that I did *not* want the reader to feel guilt. Guilt is too easy. The letter was never about white guilt; it was about the possibility of white vulnerability. But notice how a request for vulnerability turns again into an act of "race baiting," and how I am, yet again, a "piece of shit." I'm said to have "a chip on my shoulder" and I want to "justify my hatred." What hatred? The letter was a gift. The writer even makes it clear to me (in all capital letters) that *nobody* white gives a fuck what I think. He speaks on behalf of *all* white people and with such certainty. Again, I'm called a "bullshitter," but this writer's only regret is that he didn't hear my "bullshit" in person so that he could call me a "fucking nigger" to my face. He actually feels remorse, disappointment, sorrow because he wasn't able to call me a "fucking nigger" to my face? I'm also, apparently, a "worthless bitch." But wait, there is more remorse: he would like to have kicked my Black ass until I was half dead. What does this say about the world that he comes from, one in which he regrets having not left me half dead? What does this say about the anti-Black violence in white America? And what does "half dead" look like? There are times when death is probably preferable to some forms of being left half dead. And then there is the infamous use of "boy."

Other white writers, on a white racist website, also suggested that violence and death were what I deserved, with the third one having been sent directly to my university email address.

"In a sane world, this ugly nigger would be just beheaded ISIS style. Make America WHITE Again."

"This Nigger needs to have a meat hook lovingly, well, you know, time to use your own imagination!"

"Kill Yourself. Do it Immediately."

How do I reconcile myself to a country within which no doubt so many white people feel this way about me and other Black bodies? "Beheaded?" "In a 'sane' world?" "A meat hook?" "Make America WHITE Again?" At least the next writer leaves my fate in my own hands. I am told to commit suicide. Or as another writer recommended, though after meeting one condition, "Dear 'Prof' Yancy: GFY [Go Fuck Yourself] and die." Thank you. Let me again remind white readers of this book, this is twenty-first-century white America. This is your cruelty and your twisted desires—not mine. And what the hell does it mean to do something to me "lovingly" with a meat hook, and then be asked to use your own white imagination? The reality is that any one of the sickening and violent messages that I've provided above may have been written by a white person whose path I crossed earlier today, last week, a year ago; or, whose path I might cross a year from now. That is what it means to be Black in America. It means to cross the path of a white person, and not know that for them you are nothing but a nigger or that they would like to kick your Black ass and leave you half dead. Bear in mind that I'm not thinking about self-proclaimed white supremacists, I'm thinking about those white people who would never think of wearing a white pointed hood or displaying a swastika. How do I reconcile myself to this terrible and terrifying white world in which I continue to be no more than a nigger, no more than the sum of white fear, white hate, white threats, and white repugnant desire?

Never, ever say to me again that the election of Obama is proof that America is no longer despicably racist. Most of this horrid stuff that I received was sent to me when he was still in office. My fear now is that many of these same whites feel more encouraged (sanctioned, even) to be themselves given the election of Trump and his perpetuation of white nativism.

I was clearly reminded by many readers of whose country this is.

"Yeah, we white people are such awful racists. I advise the author of this piece to feel free to leave whatever white country he's stuck in and go live in any number of nonwhite countries in the world, where, no doubt, the people are so much better. We'll even help you pack."

"He should fuck off to Africa if he doesn't like living in a white country."

"Yancy, flights leave for Africa every day, take one and take a 'brutha' with you. We can all admit bringing you to this country was a mistake, so let us get rid of you and correct the mistake. You are not happy, we are not happy with your behavior, so do it."

"There are two ways you can return to Africa: On a passenger ship, or in a coffin freighter. Choose quickly."

"Your discomfort is your limited intuition telling you to GET THE FUCK OUT. Africa is calling you!"

"You're going back to Africaaaaaa!"

"Why doesn't this idiot just move to some sub-Saharan African country, where he can be around nothing but black people, for the rest of his life?"

"Deport him to Africa to ponder racism there."

Having come to the end of this chapter, perhaps there are some of you who feel speechless by the sheer magnitude and severity of white racist responses I received. In fact, you might be shocked that any letter that attempts to reach across our racial chasm to create forms of openness and honesty on the part of white people would have received such vile responses. I know that there will be some of you who will say that you were unaware of this poison that had the audacity to erupt in response to my gift of love. Now that I have shared so many of these depraved responses, you can no longer say that you are not aware.

In this chapter, I refused to be silent; there was no other real choice. First, the weight of Black pain and suffering suffused my consciousness and my conscience. Courageous speech or parrhesia was necessary. Second, the "postracial" narrative that white people tell themselves is in need of what

Baldwin called "a most disagreeable mirror."[62] The record is unambiguously clear, here for you to witness in all of its nasty, malicious, and cruel detail. And for those looking for a quick fix solution to what you've witnessed, I say, tarry with it, linger with it, try to understand, though this will not be easy, something of the details of what I was made to feel, to undergo. I ask you to linger as so many white people fail to engage the gravity of white racism as they hurry to find "solutions." Not that solutions don't matter; they do. But the rush to find them can function as a way of avoiding what is truly at stake; moreover, the rush carries the potential seduction of locating you in the role of the white "hero" or "heroine." And I assure you, there are already too many of those.

I'm with Baldwin on this one. The question that white America *must* face is why did you, *white people*, need the nigger in the first place? Baldwin says that white people simply need *to face* that question. My reconciliation with this country, the reconciliation of Black bodies with this country, this "Sweet land of liberty," will remain hollow until white America, white people are able to face that question. For this "sweet land" will remain bitter and "liberty" a mere farce without white people first facing that question, without white people coming to risk themselves, to give themselves over to the truth that they, you, are the nigger, not me. Like Baldwin, I have no use for the term nigger, but you do. I know that I'm *not* a nigger. Nigger is not my name. Baldwin's words are as painfully relevant and prophetic as they were when he said them in 1963 to African American psychologist Kenneth Clark. Thus, I end this chapter with Baldwin's powerful insight and inimitable wisdom:

> What white people have to do is try and find out in their own hearts why it was necessary to have a nigger in the first place, because I'm not a nigger. I'm a man, but if you think I'm a nigger, it means you need it. The question you've got to ask yourself—the white population of this country has got to ask itself. . . . If I'm not a nigger here and you invented him—you, the white people, invented him—then you've got to find out why. And the future of the country depends on that, whether or not it's able to ask that question . . . *simply to face that question, face that question.*[63]

RISKING THE
WHITE SELF

L et's clear a space for mutual understanding, make way for greater conceptual and communicational clarity. And like in the letter, as I suggested, let's strive for something more daring like mutual vulnerability. I
think that many white readers completely misunderstood the conceptual
scope, content, and aim of my letter. While trying to be charitable here,
many, actually most, of the responses to my letter from white readers had
to do with their failure or refusal to risk their white selves, to be touched by
the letter's weight and message of urgency, its message of love. Given the
similar tone of anger, defensiveness, and denial, it was as if white readers
came together to formulate how best to respond to a letter asking for far too
much white accountability. James Baldwin writes, "People always seem to
band together in accordance to a principle that has nothing to do with love,
a principle that releases them from personal responsibility."[1]

The majority of white readers who responded didn't tarry with the message, with the discomfort that the letter was designed to create. I understand
that the letter was bold, but in this time of racist toxicity, which has always
been the reality in America, we can't afford to be silent, indifferent, or
timid. Candid, truthful, and honest speech is necessary when it comes to
race in America, which, when it comes to white people, raises all sorts of
painful anxieties. Yet such candid and truthful speech creates a space for
crucial opportunities for white people to engage in risking the self and the
possibility for constructive transformation, something that is often painful.
In Dear White America, I came with a gift, a most disagreeable mirror, that
refused to lie about whiteness. To borrow the powerful words of Audre

Lorde, "I have come to believe over and over again that what is most important to me must be spoken, made verbal and shared, even at the risk of having it bruised or misunderstood."[2]

The concept of "white fragility," which I mentioned earlier, helps within this context. Robin DiAngelo writes, "White people in North America live in a social environment that protects and insulates them from race-based stress."[3] She continues, "This insulated environment of racial protection builds white expectations for racial comfort while at the same time lowering the ability to tolerate racial stress, leading to what I refer to as White Fragility."[4] Let me make it clear, white readers, that the concept of white fragility is not meant to appease you. That's not my reading of the concept. The concept is not to be taken as a motivation for why I should tiptoe around the issue of race when raising it in your presence, walk as if on eggshells. Try not to take offense, but your white fragility—which I would add is your way of remaining "innocent," of refusing to be vulnerable, of ignoring Black pain and suffering—*is killing us*. And I don't mean this as a metaphor. The fact of the matter is that you are not always stressed by race, because, after all, you deploy race when it best suits you, which is generally when we are the target of that deployment. The deep social, psychological, and existential stress that we endure every day of our lives, partly because your whiteness structures and saturates so many aspects of the public spaces that we must engage out of necessity, is predicated upon your racial comfort, which I see as your fundamental failure to live a life of daring, of risk, of a form of love that is capable of removing the lies that you attempt to conceal, the masks that you wear. This is *your* problem, a *white* problem. Yet because you don't see it, fail to see it, or refuse to see it, or see it and just don't give a damn, we suffer, we fail to breathe, and many of us stop breathing, literally, because of your ethical ineptitude, your refusal to love with audacity. For me, there is a relationship between the lie that whiteness is and the lies that it conceals and the power of love to challenge and begin to dismantle those lies. "To know love," as bell hooks writes, "we have to tell the truth to ourselves and to others."[5] She continues, "Creating a false self to mask fears and insecurities has become so common that many of us forget who we are and what we feel underneath the pretense. Breaking through this denial is always the first step in uncovering our longing to be honest and clear."[6]

I get it. Within a country that is predicated upon white supremacy and white normativity (where white is considered the standard), despite the fact that many white people continue to deny the contemporary reality of both, whiteness functions as a way of evading reality, as a site of security, allowing for very little slippage. Think about white normativity in this way. It is so taken for granted that it is like breathing. You just do it. Whiteness, as a site of normativity, means that it is unmarked, unraced, unnamed. As white you are deemed "normal." Yet as Black, I am marked, named, raced, and deemed "different" and "deviant." In fact, whiteness as normative, because of its taken-for-granted reality, is not the sort of thing from which you can just assume a stance of moral distance; you are that site.

The problem, though, is that white supremacy, white normativity, white power and privilege are not benign; they are toxic, malignant, deadly. Your insulation from confronting your whiteness comes at an ugly and terrible price—you live a diminished and truncated life of what it means to be truly human, and we are reminded constantly that our humanity doesn't matter. But then again, within white supremacy, our humanity is a misnomer. We were never quite human, perhaps even never really meant to exist, despite the fact that your existence as *white* depends upon your distance from us as *Black*. In fact, where would you be without us? Where would you be without the false and ugly construction of us that you have used to insulate you from engaging in an honest and truthful confrontation with your own ugly history, your own whiteness? Lorde writes, "For to survive in the mouth of this dragon we call America, we [Black women and men] have had to learn this first and most vital lesson—that we were never meant to survive. Not as human beings."[7] Whether you know it or not, whiteness is an expression of misanthropy. The white racist violation of our humanity is the story of Black life in America. That is the story of this letter writer who would dare to be human, who would dare to ask you to confront your whiteness, your inhumanity.

After I received so much hate mail, a colleague of mine said, "What if you had actually written the letter in anger?" He was bringing attention to the fact that this wasn't a letter written in anger, but one written with hope, respect, and a type of love that is daring in its removal of masks. Given the white hatred and white threats of violence that I actually received, it would seem that his question was irrelevant. You see, I'm trapped either way. If I write a letter that speaks of gift-giving and love, white folk become violent.

If I write a letter expressing ire about the state of white America, well, I become the uncontrollable, angry Black man. In the end, more hate mail, more white threats of physical violence. And as you've seen, having a PhD doesn't really give me any cachet at all. This brings us back to the reality that for me there are no exceptions. Fanon writes, "No exception was made for my refined manners, or my knowledge of literature, or my understanding of the quantum theory."[8]

Having been boxed-in by whiteness, perhaps it would have been best to have remained silent, refused to have written Dear White America. Silence, however, can also function as a kind of death. And I refuse to die. Keep in mind, though, that there are certain forms of death that are necessary. The oppressive machinations of whiteness must die so that white people (*you*) can truly live. What is meant by this death? It involves an opening, a risk, a fissure. As white, you must be open to a kind of death—a death of your stubbornness, a death of your denials, a death of your "innocence," a death of your arrogance, a death of your racial comfort, a death of your narcissism, a death of your "goodness," a death of your fears, a death of your color evasion, a death of your self-righteousness, a death of your sense of entitlement, a death of your illusions of safety, a death of your sense of "greatness" and "manifest destiny," a death of all of those tricks that you play to convince yourselves that you are fine, that you are the good ones, the sophisticated ones, the nonracist ones, the ones who truly care about justice and a world without oppression, hatred, and racist violence.

Had Dear White America been read in the spirit of what I'm referring to as a risk, a kind of death, much of what was misunderstood about my letter may have been avoided. I say "may have" because whiteness is so intractable; it is structurally opaque and insidious. For example, there were a few responses that I received from white people that implied that my letter could not have been written with them in mind because their relationship to Black people belies my point regarding their white racism. Hence, some white folk mentioned their Black friends, Black people who are part of their extended families, and one white person responded to my letter saying that she did not have time to read my letter as she was, as I recall, putting her Black grandchildren to bed. I get the point. You have Black friends; you even have Black family members whom you love. I understand that. But this doesn't free you from white racism. How you treat a few Black people in your life doesn't free you from the ways in which these Black people can function for you as *Black exceptions* in your life. In fact, if this is true and they are Black exceptions, your racism is the source of that distinction. Hence, loving a few Black people is not proof that you have confronted your own racism. And your love certainly does not remove you from the ways in which white privilege is a structural reality. No matter how much you love your Black friends or your Black partner, or your Black grandchildren or even your Black children, you are white and as such you reap the benefits of that whiteness in ways that, even if unintentional, negatively impact Black bodies.

Let us get something straight. If you've read the previous chapter, you may not discover yourself there. My guess is that you won't. Fair enough. You would never call me, nor anyone else, a nigger. The word "Coon" is not even part of your vocabulary. And you believe in the humanity of Black people, especially having never, ever given thought to the idea that Black people are monkeys or closer to monkeys than, say, white people. In short, you are not like those white supremacists. I get it. Yet as white, there are goodies to be reaped, and your hands are not totally clean. Speaking of contemporary white supremacist organizations, Jessie Daniels writes:

> In many ways, the presence of white supremacist organizations and their discourse functions to confirm the social order for whites in much the same fashion that, in another historical context, lynching—violence directed primarily at Black men—functioned. Even those not implicated, those who may have been appalled by such "vulgar" displays, still reaped the rewards of living in a system in which being born white was a social condition vastly privileged over being born Black. That white supremacists periodically act on these beliefs only confirms what many people of color already know about life in a white supremacist context—their lives are in danger.[9]

Let's face it. The love that you have for certain Black people will not protect them from the white surveillance practice of stop-and-frisk, or from being mistaken as someone "up to no good," or as someone pulling out a "weapon." Bonding with certain Black people does not exempt you from white racism, just as having married a woman does not free me from sexism. Do you really think that because I love my wife this means that I'm not sexist? Hell, many if not most marriages are predicated on patriarchy. Is that not sexist enough? Also, recall that it was Barack Obama who provided a personal testimony regarding his white grandmother where he described her as someone who loved him and sacrificed for him, but added that she was "a woman who once confessed her fear of black men who passed by her on the street, and who on more than one occasion has uttered racial or ethnic stereotypes that made me cringe."[10] The point here is that even as she no doubt affectionately looked into the eyes of her phenotypically dark grandson and taught him about duty, love, respect, and compassion, she was petrified by Black male bodies (like mine or your Black male child or Black male grandchildren) that passed her on the street. My guess is that she characterized them as "niggers." I can't be sure if she used the word nigger. Yet, does it really matter? Whatever she said about other Black males in young Obama's company, there is still the impact that this would have had on Obama. The term nigger is the harshest term created to dehumanize Black people. Yet as Taine Duncan notes, "It is part of a sliding scale on which all whites participate in racial stereotyping. Unconscious bias on one end, using the n-word on the other, but these are differences of degree and not kind."[11] Hence, whatever stereotyping Obama's white grandmother used, and while not used against Obama himself, it would still have had some type of wounding impact on him.

Lillian Smith, who writes with incredible honesty and insight about what it means to grow up white in the American South, notes, "The mother who taught me what I know of tenderness and love and compassion taught me also the bleak rituals of keeping Negroes in their 'place.' "[12] She also notes that she learned that it is possible "to pray at night and ride a Jim Crow car the next morning and to feel comfortable in doing both."[13] In America, white racism complicates the simplicity of what one would think should be a disjunction. Rabbi Abraham Joshua Heschel is aware of this complexity where he writes, "one may be decent and sinister, pious and sinful."[14] Notice the conjunction. I'm sure that this is why it was crucial for Heschel to note that "One's integrity must constantly be examined,"[15] and that "self-assurance, smug certainty of one's honesty [is] as objectionable as brazen dishonesty."[16] Smith puts her finger on the duplicity of whiteness when she writes, "Something [is] wrong with a [white] world that tells you that love is good and people are important and then forces you to deny love and to humiliate [Black] people."[17]

When I was a child, I was told that I was as good as any white person, though I was also told that I would have to work twice as hard (perhaps three times) if I was to succeed. This is something that many Black children are told. While Black parents are well-intended, and certainly mine were, notice how whiteness subtly functions as the standard in terms of which I was "as good as." In fact, given the history of white racism, it sounds counterintuitive to say to white children that they are as good as any Black person. The important point here, however, is that given the pervasive assumption that white people are "superior" to Black people and people of color, it is imperative that Black parents impart powerful messages to their Black children, messages that are designed to militate against possible forms of self-doubt and to counter white lies about Black "inferiority." It is the sort of painful realism that Black children must be told, and that I must share with my children.

I am sure that if you are white, this advice was *not* communicated to you. You see, this is partly what it means to be white. If you are to succeed, you are told to work hard as such, not harder than Black people. You are taught about the "truths" of meritocracy, of rugged individualism. You have even been told about how your forebears came to this country and worked their fingers to the bone to make it and that had it not been for that "boot-strapping" you would not be where you are today. There was no mention of whiteness, but just hard work and effort. Having been told that all you have to do is to work hard, there is the assumption that there will be no unfair and unjust *racial* competition—where Black people are at the top of the social hierarchy and will work to keep you oppressed. Of course, you could have been deceived into thinking that some Black person or person of color will more than likely "steal *your* job." Your job? Yes, the job that was meant only for you. That is white entitlement.

Some white students have told me that they have been told by their white parents that they are no better than anyone else. That we (all people) are all the same. That is so dishonest and such a damn lie! This raises Heschel's point about the need for constant examination of one's integrity. Such an assurance by white parents is not just misleading, but it obfuscates the reality of white racism. It is true that white people are in no way *inherently* better than Black people or people of color; and I mean this intellectually, morally, aesthetically, you name it. Yet there is a lie embedded within what sounds like an ethical truism. The fact of the matter is that as a white person your white parents failed, more than likely, to mention (refused to mention) how you will benefit from white privilege, even if you are poor.

Your white parents failed to tell you that your whiteness carries extraordinary value; it opens doors, and it calms white police officers. It can and does save your life. It is what you will see when you go to most movies—white people falling in love, white people being happy, white people singing and dancing in major musicals, white families in crisis, white angst, white people struggling with terminal illnesses, and white people bonding with other white people, where Black people and people of color function as background. You will see important white people in history books; white people will be your teachers, your professors, your supervisors, your minister on Sunday morning, your loan officer, the guy who owns the bank, and the company that you work for.

Like many of my white students, you probably took your parents' advice to heart, and you think that you are no better than Black people or people of color. But that you think so does not remove the fact that in white America you exist both within a de facto racially divided society and one where your life is valued differently from Black lives. And lest you think that this can't be true because you live in a racially integrated neighborhood, your whiteness still matters differently within that "integrated" space. You are still part of the white symbolic order that deems you more valuable vis-à-vis Black lives. When was the last time that you had to shout, "White Lives Matter!"? As such, what your parents told you will be contradicted by how you are treated precisely in virtue of you being white. Your whiteness, even if unknown to you, will function as an affordance, allowing for action opportunities, a range of possibilities. Indeed, your whiteness, and I'm sure that you would rather not hear this, perpetuates, whether you intend it or not, white privilege and white supremacy, both of which reinforce each other. The truth is that by the time you realize that something has gone awry within our white racist polity, white racism has already etched its way into your psyche and become part of your very embodiment. Recognizing how whiteness is a location, an embodied one, Adrienne Rich writes that to locate herself in her body "means more than understanding what it has meant to me to have a vulva and clitoris and uterus and breasts. It means recognizing this white skin, the places it has taken me, the places it has not let me go."[18] And as Smith writes, "These ceremonials in honor of white supremacy," which involve the various ways in which whiteness is deemed superior and is respected, "performed from babyhood, slip from the conscious mind down deep into muscles and glands and become diffi-cult to tear out."[19]

These crucial dimensions of whiteness are what Dear White America attempted to communicate in fewer words. Yet it is what most of the white readers failed to understand, to admit. White readers, you fled; you sought shelter, which is what I pled against. I requested that you take a deep breath as a way of preparing you for what I thought would be difficult to hear let alone accept, which most of you didn't. In the letter, I said not to tell me how many Black friends that you have. Yet you did. I said not to tell me that I'm blaming white people for everything. Unfortunately, many of you did just that. I said not to run from your responsibility. Yet many of you abdicated. This wasn't me being arrogant or "a bombast," as one writer claimed in the comments section at The Stone, the *New York Times*. My objective was to communicate to white readers in advance that there was something that I knew about the terrain of white defensiveness, white avoid-ance. This doesn't mean, by the way, that *all* objections to my letter should be framed as examples of white defensiveness or as a failure to understand the letter.

What I told white readers not to do is partly the result of teaching about race and whiteness at predominantly white institutions of higher learning and having witnessed white students respond to issues of race and whiteness in very predictable ways. There is also knowledge that, as a Black person, one acquires as a result of occupying a specific racialized location within a white supremacist society. As bell hooks writes, "Black folks have, from slavery on, shared in conversations with one another 'special' knowledge of whiteness gleaned from close scrutiny of white people."[20] This is an impor-tant epistemological advantage that Black people possess in relationship to white ways of being, white ways of avoiding the truth about their whiteness. Robert Jensen puts it this way: "What if they [Black people and people of color] know about us [white people] what we don't dare know about our-selves? . . . What if they can see what we can't even voice?"[21] And Du Bois writes, "Of them [the souls of white folk] I am singularly clairvoyant. I see in and through them."[22] He continues, "I see the working of their entrails. I know their thoughts and they know that I know. This knowledge makes them now embarrassed, now furious! They deny my right to live and be and call me misbirth."[23]

And furious the readers of Dear White America were.

"I'll admit to the imaginary racism you think white people are guilty of when you admit that [you're] a race card playing obamalicking insane retard. Bless your fucking heart."

"[I] live in a very nice Italian/Irish neighborhood. And we don't want ANY of you living near us. You are poison to a neighborhood."

"People pay money to get an education, instead they are subjected to ass-holes like you."

"Professor Yancy, please put down the crack pipe . . . you know that it heightens your paranoia."

"Professor Yancy, all your studies have forced me to examine my self-image and my white racist mind. You clearly state that no matter what I think, I'm a racist. OK, cool. Thank you for clearing that up. Now I am forced to say, because you tell me I can say nothing else, FUCK YOU NIGGER! As always, the white guy."

In the letter, I also said to white readers not to tell me that *I'm* the racist, but they did. I came away with the impression that many white people treat the term racist like the term nigger. It was as if the two words carry the same assaultive weight and ought to involve the same level of disgust over the use of each. Well, they don't and they shouldn't. A "nigger" is a fantasy, something unreal, created by white people to serve their ends. A racist and racism are all too real, though I'm sure that many Black people would prefer that white racism was an irrational nightmare from which they will eventually awake. As white, you fear a *fantasy* of your own creation; as Black, we fear a *reality* of your own creation.[24] Both the term nigger and the condition of white racism were created by you, not us. And both are despicable. In fact, both are products of your hatred, your habits, your dispositions, your values, your ways of being. They were certainly not of our design.

The comments from many of the white readers reveal a deep misunderstanding of what white racism involves. At the slightest hint that they might be racist, let alone the direct and honest, though vulnerable, approach that I used, white people shield themselves, run for cover, and make ready for a verbal arsenal that is filled with angry attacks, revisionist history, and all manner of conflation. There is also no show of that kind of love, which bell hooks delineates, that requires that we tell the truth to ourselves and to others.

> But you presume to wear my shoes in this letter. And Sir you do not. In this letter, you are doing nothing more than racial profiling, as you are lumping an entire race into one opinion, your opinion. Is this racism?

It is true that I don't walk in the shoes of this white reader. There is much that I don't know about the reader. But do I really need to walk in the reader's shoes to know that the reader, *as white*, has a different relationship to the *structural* realities of white supremacy, white privilege, and white power than people of color? I am accused of "nothing more than racial profiling." Notice how the reader deploys a policing practice, and a centuries-old practice, that wrongly targets Black and Brown people as "suspicious," as a way of countering my point that white people benefitting from white supremacy are racist. Racial profiling is what happened to Sandra Bland and Trayvon Martin. It is what happened to Black bodies under American slavery and Jim Crow. It is a practice that presupposes an entire set of vile racist images, assumptions, and stereotypes. Within the context of white America, the practice is backed by white racist institutional structures and legal decision making that impact Black lives in deeply problematic and vicious existential ways.

To say that I am racially profiling in Dear White America is to take completely out of historical context the deeply painful and existential consequences that such racial profiling by white people entailed and entails for Black bodies. Keep in mind that historically when a Black man was accused of "raping" a white woman, it didn't matter if the man was guilty or not. In fact, *any* Black man was always already guilty. That is racial profiling. The practice speaks to deeper white psychological needs and grotesque white desires. Within this context, racial profiling is connected to the existing structure of white authority that sanctioned the carrying out of the lynching spectacle. My point is that racial profiling of Black people within white America has a long and violent history. Even if I were to grant that I "racially profiled" white people in Dear White America, which I didn't, the act itself is empty of historical precedent. There was simply no extant, widespread antiwhite violence, the subjugation of white people by Black people in the form of legalized slavery, brutalization, and dehumanization.

When I spoke of white racism in my letter, and more specifically, the white racism of white people reading the letter, my aim was to get white people to *rethink* how they think about racism, their racism. It was an attempt to introduce different ways of seeing the world and encouraging white people to see themselves differently in relationship to that world, especially the ways in which they are embedded within a white supremacist world in which they perpetuate and benefit from that world. This is not a case of "lumping an entire race." Indeed, I never used the term race as a so-called biological category to address white America. Is it *my* opinion, as the reader says? Not if the reader means that it is something that only I hold to be true, something silly that I've cooked up, something that has no objective basis outside of what I think. The reader asks, "Is this racism?" My answer is, "No!"

Calling someone a racist is name calling.

Within the context of Dear White America, this is simply false. Name calling is the act of calling someone an offensive name that is intended to hurt, harm, degrade, or humiliate. Did many white people treat my use of the term racist as an offensive term? Certainly. I'm sure that when I call men sexist, many of them would say that the term is offensive. However, treating the term racist or sexist as offensive doesn't make the application of the term false. By reducing my use of the term racist to one of "name calling," the reader implies that my aim was to hurt. I wonder if the reader would have said I was name calling if I had said that the Ku Klux Klan is racist. Probably not. While I could be wrong here, the reader wants to deflect the complexity with which I used the term racist in Dear White America. In my view, many white people are lovers of justice and believers in fairness, but this doesn't free them from the intricate ways in which they perpetuate and benefit from white supremacy. My aim was to share a gift, to engage in mutual openness, a mutual daring to look deeper and wider in terms of how white people are ensconced within a *system* of oppression, one that favors them, and how they have internalized, even if unconsciously, forms of white racist poisoning. For the record, I have had my fill of name calling. As one white reader communicated when referring to me on one website, "Cunts like this aren't philosophers, they just hate white people, simple."

> Your gift is a pernicious one. Telling me that I am no more than my race doesn't invite me to grow. Telling me that I am no better than the worst of my kind doesn't coax me from my herd. I can think of no better way to alienate would-be allies. King invited me to become something better. You tell me I'm something less.

Well, I did say in the letter that some gifts can be heavy to bear. But why was it perceived as pernicious or evil? And, again, I take issue with the assumption underlying what the reader means by "race." To commit to the claim that one is no more than his/her "race" is to support reductionist assumptions about "race" that are indicative of white racist thinking throughout the history of Europe and America. For example, as Black, as being a member of a certain racial group (call it "Negroid"), I'm deemed "inferior"; I am *no more* than my race. And I would assure the white reader, and any white reader reading this book, that Black people are painfully aware of how such assumptions don't "invite" us to grow. More painfully, Black people were not only not "invited" to grow, but we were oppressed, taught that we were "stupid," "ugly," and meant to be "slaves for life," in order to destroy any aspiration to grow. And to keep us in "our place" (assuring us that we were no more than our race), we were brutally beaten and killed as a consequence of trying to be more than white people stipulated. Surely, this is not what I'm doing in Dear White America. In fact, there was an invitation to grow. To encourage white people to understand how they benefit from structures of white racist power that are historically grounded, pervasive, subtle, and often invisible to them, is actually an encouragement to enlarge their consciousness and to see the world with greater clarity, especially in terms of its complexity. That is not pernicious.

The white reader's discourse of "my kind," which I don't use, is again reductionist. There is no "my kind." However, there are people who we recognize as "white" and who thereby have a different relationship to a country that is predicated upon white supremacy. I am concerned with the discursive and structural forces that made it possible for some people to "become white," and thereby come to occupy supposedly the "apex" of humanity and civilization, not with "my kind" or "your kind." That is too fixed. The white reader also implies that I hold that he/she is no better than "the worst of my kind." I assume that the reader is saying that I hold that he/she as white is no better than, say, the KKK. In Dear White America, I never made such a claim. What is evident to me is the white reader's desire that there should be a clear distinction between "good white people" and the "bad ones" (the KKK). There is also a sense of anger that I'm implicating non-self-avowed white supremacist white people in the perpetuation of white supremacy, white privilege, white power.

One white reader wrote what felt very sincere: "If I invited you to dinner, would you still sit in my home and call me racist?" Look, let's be clear. I have plenty of white friends. Are they members of the KKK? No. Do these white friends reap the benefits of white privilege, white power, and the history of white supremacy? Are they intelligent, decent human beings? Do they fight against white racism? Yes, yes, and yes again. Do I consider these friends to be racist? Yes. There is nothing contradictory in that statement. Being a white antiracist and yet being a racist are not mutually exclusive. For me, the "good white people" versus the "bad white people" functions for both of these white readers in such a way that it shifts and avoids the message of the letter—look at *your* racism. Daniels makes a similar point where she argues that nationally syndicated shows that have brought on white supremacist groups have created a distinction that sidelines important forms of self-interrogation by white viewers. She writes, "Talk-show audiences are alerted to tune in to 'see what racists are like.' Framing the appearance of white supremacists in this way preempts any other interrogation of racism by the audience, the host, or society at large."[25]

Also, I wasn't trying to "coax" white people from their "herd." My letter was aimed at white people who are embedded within a system, not racist whites as opposed to nonracist whites. I had hoped that Dear White America would create more white allies, not to alienate them. I have had readers of my larger body of work, or who have heard me speak, suggest that I would probably get more white people to listen to me if I didn't use the term racist to describe them. "Yancy, they wouldn't shut down so fast if you just stop saying that they are racists." But what would I gain? Do I really have time for a placated white ally, a white ally who agrees with me just as long as his/her sensibilities are not offended? Given the brutal history of white racism and its insidious and fatal contemporary manifestations, why appease white people, why cut them slack? They have had centuries to collectively change the course of white American brutality toward Black people, to collectively face their racism. Look, I refuse to appease *Black people* about what it means to be Black in white America; appeasement can easily cost them their life. I refuse to cut corners. "In America, you are considered a nigger!" And when my children forget, they must be reminded. Of course, Baldwin is also right there in my back pocket, "You can only be destroyed by believing that you really are what the white world calls a *nigger*."[26] I remind them of how they are perceived, at the same time making damn sure that they do not believe that this is what they are.

I certainly refuse to appease white people who contribute to making Black life a living hell. White people must begin to understand and feel the weight of responsibility for those Black people and people of color who live under the yoke of their whiteness. Within the context of white supremacy, one's whiteness doesn't float above the muck and mire of practices that oppress Black bodies, but fundamentally "links to" and impacts those bodies. I am sexist; one who fights daily against his sexism and the system that supports this. My sexism is also a kind of yoke. I suspect that my openness makes for a different kind of ally to women. Let's assume that it doesn't. Well, that is fine with me, because at the end of the day I want a world in which women don't suffer from sexist structures of domination. I want a world in which women are not sexually harassed within the work place or outside of it, a world in which women are not reduced to sexual objects, sexual toys, grabbed by their "pussies," expected to do "us" sexual favors for promotion, assumed to want and desire our uninvited sexual advances. But let's be careful. What we are witnessing at this moment in American history, regarding the sexual harassment charges against high-profile male figures, is just scratching the surface. Women who suffer under structural and systemic forms of subjugation due to their gender, race, class, disability, and sexuality, are not being heard adequately. Their voices remain silenced. As men, we have collectively failed women; we have failed ourselves by not interrogating a conception and a system of masculinity and power that violates the integrity of women's lives, their desires, their self-understanding. Because I'm able to point this out, however, doesn't provide me with clean hands. I don't want to be coaxed into accepting a critical feminist approach to patriarchy by being told that I'm one of the "good ones." My objective is not to propitiate women, but to take ownership of my sexism and my male privilege, even as it is complicated by race, and to make a difference in terms of how I treat women and trouble the systemic structure of patriarchy.

The reader is on target with the King reference. At least she didn't leave the following message in my university inbox, as one white writer did:

> FUCK you. Hater. Dr. King would be ashamed of you and your kind.

Or, as another white reader wrote as late as March 2017:

> How dare you. My kids are Puerto Rican. Wife is Indian. Best friends are black. You label someone sir a racist. MAKES YOU ONE. Poor MLK. He would be ashamed of your people as you say. You['re] not fit to educate anyone if it's hate.

King did invite white people to be something better. In fact, and this quote may surprise many white people, King said, "I am sorry to have to say that the vast majority of white Americans are racists, either consciously or unconsciously."[27] Apparently, this is the same King who, according to the one writer, would be ashamed of me. Keep in mind that the vast majority of white people, then and now, are not KKK members.

Finally, I didn't want less from white people, as the reader accuses, but far more. I wanted white readers to begin to think differently about their whiteness within a complex and fluid relational context. As Ladelle McWhorter writes, "When I say I want to think differently, I mean I want to live differently, and that means dismantling old habits and developing new ways of behaving and moving and interacting and perceiving."[28]

> I have a gift for you "Professor," but it may not be easy to hear. Judging an entire race based upon the color of their skin is the definition of racism. Martin Luther King, Jr. once said, "I look to a day when people will not be judged by the color of their skin, but by the content of their character." This is the ideal to which you should strive, but instead you look only at color and judge an entire group based upon your own color and judge an entire group based upon your own pre-conceived notions. Racism will never disappear as long as it is condoned by those who should know better.

This white reader's opening comments mimic my letter. The part of the response that isn't easy for me to hear, however, is the reader's deflationary concept of racism. When I say that as a male within a patriarchal system I'm sexist and that as a white person in a white supremacist system white people are racist, I am not being racist, I am pointing to the ways in which white people are relationally situated within a white systemic power structure and the ways in which white people as a result have come to internalize racist beliefs, images, and affects. This is not judging a group based on the color of their skin, but how the white supremacist system has constituted white people according to the complex power relationships endemic to that system. White people in Europe and America judged people based upon the color of their skin, and for Black people the judging came with oppressive and deadly consequences. The concept of race as a category that carries all types of false conceptual content, distorted assumptions, vicious lies, and profound normative implications came out of Europe and America. In this sense, race is a category that is historically inextricably linked to oppressive power relationships. And the act and process of judging was supported by white institutions and white ideologies, white sites of "knowledge" production. King would have certainly been against this. In fact, he gave his life fighting against white supremacy, which is a system, not simply an attitude or a false belief.

At no point did I say that the color of your skin *makes* you a racist. This was and is the type of reasoning embedded within white American racism. Judgments based upon my skin color made me "fit" for riding in the Jim Crow car, "qualified" me for drinking out of the Colored Only fountain, forced me to attend racially separate and unequal schools, made me sit at the back of the bus, exposed me to the control mechanisms of Black codes and subjected me to convict leasing, and violently forced me to hang from a tree because I was accused of raping a white woman. That is how King understood "judging an 'entire race' based upon the color of their skin."

It is so easy for white people to retreat to a form of individualism designed to nullify their group status. But I get it, you don't want to be associated with a group. Sorry, but that resistance is a function of whiteness, white privilege. Even your talk of "individualism" and "boot-strapping" are racially coded words. They are indicative of white privilege and demonstrate how white supremacy functions. My claim that to be white in America is to be racist is a contextual claim about how your whiteness is perceived, how it has been historically constructed, how white racism is learned at the proverbial knee, and how you, despite the ways in which your subject position is a complicated one (poor, liberal, progressive, disabled, LGBTQ, you name it), reap and perpetuate white racism in subtle and not so subtle ways of being white within a white supremacist world. "A nigger," through the lens of white racism, *is* a nigger. Essentialism is explicit in the judgment. To be a white racist, in my view, doesn't imply essentialism at all.

For the record, there are many white people who use the language of King in order to move as quickly as possible beyond talking about whiteness. The objective is to use King's language to obfuscate the continued reality of racism. According to this logic, the more that I talk about race and whiteness, the more that I, as the reader implies, prevent the "ideal" that King talked about from coming to fruition. The ideal world in King's dream was one without capitalist greed, hate, violent divisiveness, poverty, war, militarism, and white supremacy. However, King's four adult children continue to be judged based on the color of their skin even fifty years since his assassination. We can't even begin to talk about King's dream without white people being prepared to risk themselves and actually engage in a serious and honest discussion about deep forms of opaque racism and continued white structural power and privilege.

The white writer implies that I am a person who condones racism and that I should know better. In fact, according to the reader, racism will never disappear because of my actions. Contrary to this reader's claim, pointing out how white people continue to benefit from white supremacy and how they are part of a *system* that treats them differently from Black people and people of color is not racist. If Black people historically had the power, the institutional and legal means, the hatred and the will to act on that hatred to oppress you in virtue of your being white, my hope is that I would stand with you, that I would be your ally. Then again, unfortunately, and as asinine and contradictory as this would be, like you, perhaps I would call you *the racist* when you pointed to *my racism* within that system.

George Yancy is promoting the idea that I'm a racist because of my race (which is itself a racist construct), and that there is nothing that I can do to change that.

Again, the first part of this reader's comment is problematic in the ways that I've just pointed out. At no point did I say that there is nothing that a white person can do about being a racist. For me to have committed to such a claim would belie the important reason for writing the letter. In fact, calling out your racism, and trying to get you to call it out and to risk your "white innocence," was coupled with my desire that you imagine the impact that such honesty might have on you and the world. Such a claim opens up the future for rich possibilities in terms of how white people might come to nurture ungated imaginations[29] and work toward a world without white supremacy, white power, and white privilege. This same misconception was expressed in an email message sent to me by another white reader. He wrote:

> If you are saying that white Americans are born with racism, then you sir are the racist or at least a bigot. . . . If your view of "white Americans" is that they are all racist and cannot do anything to change it, then you are racist, prejudiced, and should have no part in educating anyone else. I find your article offensive and divisive. I will pray for your soul.

The only part of this message that I accept, and eagerly so, is that he will pray for my soul. Then again, he might very well find my article "offensive" and "divisive" given his complete misunderstanding of my argument.

In an effort to provide greater conceptual clarity, it is important for me to explain what I mean by white racism. In the letter, I didn't have space to engage the complexity of how I understand white racism. The following will provide more clarity and hopefully provide a vocabulary that assists in that understanding.

When teaching courses on race and whiteness, my students and I collectively read Peggy McIntosh's important article in which she explores white and male privilege. To white readers, I highly recommend this article. I think that it will help you better understand my letter. In the article, after exploring the concept of white privilege, McIntosh gives forty-six examples. For example, in the first-person singular, she writes, "I can go shopping alone most of the time, pretty well assured that I will not be followed or harassed."[30] A significant part of what makes McIntosh's article so powerful is the way in which she conceptualizes the white self as complicit in the systemic operational power of white privilege. The white reader should note that I have had white students object to the example just given, only later to recant, realizing that they were probably stopped by security as they entered a store because of their age or attire or because of their multiple tattoos and piercings. I have never had a white student say that she has been stopped *because she is white.* And so I ask you, white readers: Have you ever been followed in a store *because you are white*?

My objective in using McIntosh's work here is to have you think about the deeper ways in which your whiteness functions to sustain and contribute to white racism, even as you are, understandably, resistant to the term "racist." McIntosh even clears a conceptual space for understanding her own white identity as racist. She writes, "In my class and place, I did not see myself as racist because I was taught to recognize racism only in individual acts of meanness by members of my own group, never in invisible systems conferring unsought racial dominance on my group from birth."[31] Like many white readers of my letter, as I have just shown, the term racist is used too narrowly, which functions to clear them (you) of any racism. Seeing herself as *not* racist is the result of a narrow understanding of racism—as a site of individual acts of meanness. Construing racism in terms of what is systemically conferred or bestowed, it follows that, for McIntosh, the extension of the term racist includes herself *and* those from her group (other whites) who are recipients of the conferral or bestowal of racial dominance from birth.

Consider a scenario where you, as a white person, walk into a store at the same time as a Black person, and the Black person is followed by a white security guard and you are allowed to shop. Perhaps as one of my white students argued, you might contend that if a person racialized as Black is followed by the white security guard that this in no way makes you the racist. Rather, it is the white security guard, the one who carries out the "individual act of meanness," the one who initiates the actual following, the one who has the racist stereotype, who is the racist. If this is your argument, like my white student, you are overlooking the way in which you are still the recipient and perpetrator of racial dominance. Indeed, the fact that you are not racially profiled and followed (because you are white) is inextricably linked to the fact that the Black person is racially profiled and followed. As white, you can walk into stores without anyone doubting the integrity of your character and intentions. As Zeus Leonardo notes, "[White] privilege is granted even without a subject's cognition that life is made a bit easier for her."[32] As white you can walk into the store on the basis of assumed innocence, but this "innocence" is linked to the Black person's assumed guilt. Recall that this is how white racism works. He/she is Black therefore he/she is a "criminal," the one who is "morally suspect." And keep in mind that although white people do commit crimes, Black people, within the context of white supremacy, *are criminals.* Barbara Applebaum writes, "Privilege also consists in the presumption of white moral integrity that is, in the larger picture, contingent upon the co-construction of [Black people] as morally suspect."[33]

The difficult part is for you, white readers, to understand the profound ways in which you are implicated in a complex network of racist power relationships, the ways in which racism constitutes what we'll call heteronomous webs of white practices to which you, as white, are linked both as a beneficiary and as a co-contributor to such practices. White racial oppression, power, and privilege can be conceptualized, though not exclusively, as uneventful acts of being white, such as walking into a store and not being followed. In this way, white racial oppression, power, and privilege are "connected to one's very being constituted as white."[34] Notice that you don't have to be one of the writers or callers who spewed all of the vile racism after reading my letter. To be white within the context of white supremacy is to be privileged, which implies a relationship of racial domination in relationship to Black people and people of color. A white student of mine once said that he accepts the view that white people have white privilege, but he couldn't accept the view that thereby white people, which included himself, dominate nonwhite others. However, because you "benefit from" white supremacy you "contribute to" white supremacy,[35] which is a relational process that has domination built into it. The student wanted to have his white privilege without accepting the oppressive consequences and implications tied to it in relationship to Black bodies.

Many scholars have addressed the ways in which racism is fundamentally linked to being white, how whiteness is itself a site of racial domination. For example, Stephanie M. Wildman and Adrienne D. Davis write:

> Because part of racism is systemic, I benefit from the privilege that I am struggling to see. . . . All whites are racist in this sense of the term, because we benefit from systemic white privilege. Generally whites think of racism as voluntary, intentional conduct, done by horrible others. Whites spend a lot of time trying to convince ourselves and each other that we are not racist. A big step would be for whites to admit that we are racist.[36]

Robert Jensen writes:

> I have struggled to resist that racist training and the racism of my culture. I
> like to think I have changed, even though I routinely trip over the lingering
> effects of that internalized racism and the institutional racism around me. But
> no matter how much I "fix" myself, one thing never changes—I walk through
> the world with white privilege. . . . White privilege is not something I get to
> decide whether I want to keep. Every time I walk into a store at the same
> time as a black man and the security guard follows him and leaves me alone
> to shop, I am benefiting from white privilege.[37]

Cynthia Kaufman writes:

> The image of the black thief helps stabilize the image of the average good
> citizen (who of course is coded as white). When I walk into a store and the
> clerks look at me with respect and assume that I am not going to steal any-
> thing, the trust that I receive is at least partially built upon the foundation of
> my distance from the image of the savage. When an African American walks
> into the store that unconscious material comes into play in the opposite way.[38]

And, bell hooks writes:

> When liberal whites fail to understand how they can and/or do embody
> white-supremacist values and beliefs even though they may not embrace rac-
> ism as prejudice or domination (especially domination that involves coercive
> control), they cannot recognize the ways their actions support and affirm the
> very structure of racist domination and oppression that they profess to wish
> to see eradicated.[39]

Each of those quotes capture an aspect of what I call the "conception of
the embedded white racist." My hope is that this idea helps you to understand the myth that when it comes to white racism, your white racism, you
are not fully autonomous, etymologically a "law" unto yourself. The idea
here is that as embedded within a preexisting social matrix of white power,
a matrix which fundamentally constitutes who you are, though not in a
deterministic way, you must critically rethink the ways in which you are *not*
a site of complete self-possession (that is, not in complete possession of
how you are constituted), but, rather, a site of dispossession[40] (that is, that

you are constituted through others, institutional and discursive forces). Part of the meaning here is that to be white is not to be a sovereign self that governs its own meaning, definition, and constitution. The white embodied self that you are is constituted through its connection to discursive and material practices that are fundamentally racist and in terms of which you are already consigned a meaning; you are an embodied white self that has already been given over, as it were, to embedded and embodied white others. Judith Butler writes, "The body has its invariably public dimension. Constituted as a social phenomenon in the public sphere, my body is and is not mine. Given over from the start to the world of others, it bears their imprint, is formed within the crucible of social life."[41]

My point here is to provide a conceptual space for you to understand how you are materially and socially linked to white racist forms of embodied and institutional practices. Like the simple act of walking into a store with (white) racial impunity/immunity, you constitute the site of white embodiment that "bears the imprint" of white silent assumptions, moral integrity, and greater freedom of bodily movement in social space. Many white people respond to this example in ways that reinforce their assumptions that they are purely autonomous selves, neoliberal subjects, and that racism is exclusively about racial stereotyping and being, in some way, mean-spirited toward the Black person, in this case, walking into the store. If this is your position, my argument challenges you to come to terms with your embeddedness within the system of white privilege and white supremacy. In this view, "All whites are responsible for white dominance since their 'very being depends on it.'"[42] In short, as white, you are constituted relationally and preconfigured in the lives of Black people and people of color, especially in ways that perpetuate white racism and that have implications for their oppression.

I understand that you didn't create the system of white supremacy, but this does not free you from perpetuating white racism, it does not free you from the ways in which you are responsible for the maintenance of white racism. Part of the problem, as Barbara Applebaum brilliantly argues,[43] is that white people presume a thin causal nexus within which racist responsibility must be directly and causally traced back to their actions for that action to qualify as racist. My point, though, is that white people fail to understand the ways in which a thick conception of the embedded white racist self, a self that is also linked to perpetuating structural injustice, high-lights their being part of a larger white racist social network of "belonging together with [white] others in a system of interdependent processes of cooperation and competition through which [whites] seek benefits and aim to realize projects."[44]

This is what I had in mind in chapter 2 where I briefly mentioned being white and being positioned systemically or structurally within a white supremacist world. So, by simply walking into a store to shop, it is *as if* you've signed an invisible contract with other white people that says that you will not be suspected of being a criminal. Yet part of that signed contract is that Black bodies will be immediately rendered suspect. Here is a case where just shopping while white, moving freely from one aisle to the next, and never thinking once that you might be stopped, has consequences for Black bodies. The simple act of moving freely through space as white has significant relationally systemic, hegemonic, and ethical implications. And as Black, as I am followed, I live under the yoke of your whiteness. The root meaning of the word yoke implies a "joining together."

I want you, white readers, to rethink the distinction between "spectacu-lar" racist events (say, a lynching) and the mundane, everyday types (like shopping); both have destructive and detrimental implications for Black bodies. I want you to consider the possibility that your white body is rela-tionally entangled with my Black body. In fact, here I want you to rethink the concept of edges in terms of our bodies. Edward S. Casey says of edges that, "They are where material substance or physical landscape comes to a finish. They are where matter peters out."[45] However, what if the process of petering out isn't as simple as say, marking the outside limit of your body? In the shopping example, as I am stopped and you get to shop, I am impacted—*touched*—by the "innocence" of your white body, by its continued free movement within the space of the store. In other words, the social space that is traversed by both of us within the space of the store, how we get to live our respective motility (that is, our ability to move about spontaneously and actively), is already part of a racialized integument (or racialized social skin) in terms of which we move. Hence, your white body, as the privileged body, is already contiguous with (touching upon) my Black body, as the disadvantaged body, within that space. Perhaps it is here that you might begin to rethink the ethical implications that follow, what I call an ethics of no edges, where whiteness as a systemic structure has negative implications for me as you move obliviously through the world. Applebaum writes, "The white complicity claim maintains that all whites, by virtue of systemic white privilege that is inseparable from white ways of being, are implicated in the production and reproduction of systemic racial injustice.[46] The emphasis is placed on "white ways of being," something pervasive and mundane. This raises questions regarding the ethical and the unethical beyond *individual intent*. Yet, as McIntosh writes, "I was taught [as a white person] to see myself as an individual whose moral state depended on her moral will."[47]

It is important that as a white person reading this book you don't assume that a critical engagement with white racism somehow places you "outside" the social matrix of whiteness with all of its messiness. As Applebaum writes, "No white person can stand outside the system"[48] of white power. And although it is true, within the context of white power and privilege, that not all whites are impacted by whiteness in the same way, "all whites," according to Barbara Trepagnier, "are infected"[49] by whiteness.

It is also important that the white reader understands what I call the "conception of the opaque white racist self." White people who responded angrily to my letter appear to have assumed that when it came to their racism, the racism that they rejected, they were able to ascertain whether or not they were racist through a sincere act of introspection. As one reader wrote, "Yancy doesn't know my heart."[50] Given the moral investment that white people place in the rhetoric of a "color-blind" United States, despite their embeddedness within systemic white racist practices, and the social stigma that they feel when labeled racist, I would argue, with Ann Berlak, that "introspection as ordinarily understood is more often an imaginative *construction* than a retrieval process."[51] That is, it is not an effective method for ascertaining the "truth" about the internal depth of one's white racism.

What I mean here is that as a white person you are unable to give an account of your "racist limits." In other words, the white racist self that you are has already been formed by white racism in fundamentally and profoundly constitutive ways, ways that are densely complex. The white self that you are, who attempts to "ascertain such limits," has already arrived too late[52] to determine the complex and insidious ways in which white racism has become embedded within your white embodied self. It is not that there is no transparency at all, that one is incapable of identifying various aspects of one's racist/nonracist white self. Rather, the reality of the sheer depth of white racialization is far too opaque.

I often use white antiracist activist Tim Wise's experience as an example to demonstrate what I mean by white racist opacity. In 2003, Wise boarded a 737 headed to St. Louis. He notes, "I glanced into the cockpit . . . and there I saw something I had never seen before in all the years I had been flying: not one but two black pilots at the controls of the plane."[53] Despite all of his antiracist work and the antiracist training that he had provided, and continues to provide, for other whites, Wise admits that he thought: "Oh my God, can these guys fly this plane?"[54] What is powerful about this disclosure is that Wise also points out that what *he knew to be true* was of little help. Despite what he knew—that is, that Black pilots are more than capable of flying planes—his racism triumphed, perhaps accompanied by deep *feelings* of trepidation, anxiety, and images of so-called perpetually incompetent Black bodies. It was not about what he knew to be true through self-reflection; rather, it was about white formative racist dynamics that exceed his so-called full self-knowledge regarding his racism. Wise's experience demonstrates how white racism is embedded within one's embodied perceptual engagement with the social world and how it is woven into, etched into, one's white psyche, forming an opaque white racist self that can impact, in deeply problematic ways, everyday mundane social transactions and engagements with Black people and people of color. Wise is already linked to the domain of otherness in the form of prior social relationships involving formative, in this case, racist influences. "Oh my God, can these guys fly this plane?" is not a disinterested inquiry, but the expression of a profoundly hidden expression of white racism. He is ambushed by the white racism etched into his white soul that is hidden from self-reflection. Of course, when it comes to white police officers, such an opaque form of white racism might cost me my life as a Black man.

My conception of the opaque white racist self and the embedded white racist self are two important concepts that point to complex ways in which, as a white person, you never clearly come to a place of "arrival"—where such a place suggests a static noun—as a *"nonracist* white." For me, just as I am an antisexist sexist, as white, you are an antiracist racist, a concept that I mentioned in chapter 2. Despite what the one white reader said about me being committed to the claim that there is nothing to be done about racism, my view about racism does not constitute a dead end from which no exit is at all possible. Rather, what I've provided briefly here are the grounds for a more robust sense of white humility and conceptual clarity regarding the complexity of white racism; it is a call for risking the white self—to tell the truth to yourselves and to others. This, according to bell hooks, as we've seen, is an act of love.

A sense of white humility is what my white students experience after completing an assignment where I give them the task of keeping a journal or diary of their everyday encounters with white racism, many of which they would have simply overlooked or interpreted as of no significant meaning for themselves or for their white friends and white family members who they are required to record. I acquired the idea for this assignment from the significant and insightful sociological work done by Joe R. Feagin and his colleagues. As Feagin writes, "I have found that much blatantly racist thought, commentary, and performance has become concentrated in the social 'backstage,' that is, social settings where only whites are present."[55] I typically instruct my students, over the course of twelve to fifteen weeks, to record anything that they witness in the "backstage" that has racist implications. Many of my white students are skeptical. They assume that their diaries will be short and sparse. However, the assignment pushes them to new levels of attentive acuity and troubles their illusions regarding white racism not being an intimate part of the fabric of their everyday existence. It is important to note that the following observations are from some of the same white students who came into my course believing that racism is a thing of the past, that we live in a "postracial" America, and that if racism does exist it is episodic and infrequent.

It is important to note that my white students' assumption that their diaries will be short and sparse is itself a function of white privilege, especially as they are not the targets of such white racism. And because they don't listen critically, or perhaps because they have become ethically immune, such racism has become a kind of default background "white noise." Given the history of white racism, white microaggressions, and white opacity, my Black students and students of color would not make the same assumption. They don't live in a world in which they are able to grant *a priori* that there will be a shortage in everyday encounters with white racism. White skepticism regarding the pervasiveness of white racism not only functions as a form of privilege, and violence that harms the epistemological agency of people of color,[56] but such skepticism can function to impede white people from pursuing a greater understanding regarding the complexity and ubiquity of white racism.

Typically, in any given semester, my white students will attempt to convince me that they constitute a new generation that has fundamentally changed when it comes to treating Black people in racist ways. They assure me that they are different from their white parents and white grandparents. I have yet to be convinced. While optimistic, I have found that my white students have not really understood the social and existential dynamics of what it means to be Black in America; they have not come to terms with white America's embedded and recalcitrant racist historical past and present. Richard Wright writes:

> I feel that for white America to understand the significance of the problem of [the vast majority of Black people] will take a bigger and tougher America than any we have yet known. I feel that America's past is too shallow, her national character too superficially optimistic, her very morality too suffused with color hate for her to accomplish so vast and complex a task.[57]

Although Wright wrote this in 1940, I would argue that his powerful characterization here is applicable to the same white America that I addressed in my letter in 2015.

As you read some of the following examples, realize that these nasty and vile white racist entries are frighteningly similar to the ones directed at me in chapter 2. And what is so scary and alarming about these entries is that they were recorded within the context of white people casually talking to other white people within white spaces, not the result of white racist vitriol directed at a Black man who wrote a challenging letter to white America. Insightfully, James Baldwin writes, "I have often wondered, and it is not a pleasant wonder, just what white Americans talk about with one another."[58] These journal entries help to answer that question. For me, and for you, these entries ought to put to rest the bad faith discourse that would have us believe that white America has made significant progress when it comes to the elimination of the color line. Consider the following:

> I was with my family and we were discussing my Super Bowl plans. My dad mentioned how he didn't want me to go downtown after the game because it could get crazy. Someone else agreed and said I shouldn't go off campus because it will be dark and there are black people.

Notice how there is a white consensus regarding what it means to remain safe. Being on campus is the "safe space," the space of predominantly white bodies. Being off campus, especially when it's *dark*, places one's white body in imminent danger. After all, there will be *Black people* there. And notice how "it could get crazy" smoothly transitions to Black people and darkness.

> I was sitting in my guy friends' room while they watched a movie. One friend poured half his Monster energy drink into a cup for another friend. I told him I was taking a sip, grabbed the glass, and did so. When I sat the glass back down he looked mortified. I asked what was wrong and he pointed to saliva left on the side of the glass and replied, "You nigger-lipped it!"

The root meaning of the term mortify means to kill, cause death. This guy was clearly devastated by her sip, which left saliva. That alone could have been the cause for distress. In this case, having "nigger-lipped it" raises the event to the level of a specific *racialized* and *racist* disgust or repulsion.

> I was out to dinner with my friend and my text message notification went off on my cell phone. My ringtone is a P. Diddy song, and my friend, joking around, said, "I didn't know you liked nigger music."

One can only wonder how many of these nasty insults are excused as "joking around" within all white spaces. "Nigger music" is music produced by "niggers." The message is clear. There is music as such and then there is that "nigger noise."

> Yesterday alone I can count many instances where I heard the word nigger, or a variation (niglet, nig-nog, nig). I was playing video games with my friend, not of African American background, and he would say the word nigger after throwing an interception or when I would score. Another instance was when I received a text message from my friend, also a Caucasian, and after I answered his question, he said, "Alright, thanks nig nog."

"Yesterday alone"? This is revealing. Use of the term nigger is not seasonal. It is a staple of white discourse, which means a staple of white ways of constructing and making sense of their lived space—making sense of "me."

I went to get my nails done with one of my friends, and while we were picking out our nail polish colors I asked her what she thought of a dark purple. Jokingly, she said that that dark of a nail polish would make my nails look like nigger nails.

Jokingly? The subtext is that "nigger nails," or the semblance thereof, is something to be abhorred. And there is darkness as a trope for Black people or "niggers." This raises an entire category of things to be detested— "nigger feet," "nigger lips," "nigger babies," and "nigger sex." Oh, wait, the last one here is not as clear cut within the white imaginary. After all, "nigger sex" is something to be detested and yet to be coveted.

A couple of friends and I were talking about guys we liked. One girl had a black guy who asked for her number. She said she was afraid because he was so intimidating, so she gave it to him. Later on in the conversation, she said she could never marry him because "if we had kids, I wouldn't know how to take care of their hair."

Here is a white woman who is so afraid of a Black guy that she literally gives him her number. She gave him her real phone number? I have been told by women that they have indeed felt intimated when men speak to them. They fear that not responding to men's advances might incite humiliating name calling. I have every reason to believe women in this case. In fact, women often feel that they will be the recipient of physical violence within such contexts. But why her real number? Also, because she is describing a "black guy," the intimidation experienced cannot simply be separated from the racialization of the encounter. This is a case of the Black male body as terrifying, which is reminiscent of the racist symbolism within the movie *King Kong* where white actress Fay Wray is horrified by the sight of Kong. Then she later moves to the subject of marriage, not even entertaining the idea of dating first. Even so, there will be no marriage. After all, there is that unmanageable "nigger hair." Even as she feels intimated, she has the time to consider marriage and to assess the racist basis upon which there would be no marriage?

My friend and I were discussing ways to become rich. She suggested that she should adopt an African baby so he will be a sports star and share his millions with her once he grows up.

Back to stereotypes. In this case, there is the racist assumption of the "naturally athletic" Black body. What happens when, God forbid, she does adopt and he is lousy at playing all sports? Perhaps she can return the purchased item and say that it was defective, not really Black or Black enough.

> Last night, a group of friends were drinking in [M] and [G]'s room. I picked up a stuffed raccoon off of [G]'s bed. One of the boys in the room said, "Oh [M], that's something you and [G] have in common: you both sleep with coons."

The subtext here is frightening. Coon refers to the way in which Black people were compared to raccoons. In short, Black people are deemed subhuman animals. This means that the two white girls have a rather perverse desire to engage in acts of bestiality.

> One white girl was talking about why she could not date a black guy and she mentioned the black hands. "When they turn over their hand, that is really gross—they look like gorillas' hands."

This white girl isn't intimidated. And she is not worried about the difficulty of taking care of "nigger hair." She is disgusted by those gross "gorilla hands" of Black guys. Perhaps she even gets sick to the stomach when she thinks about dating Black guys, and having those "gorilla hands" touching her "precious" and "civilized" white skin. We are back to the primitive, back to Skull Island, and back to King Kong. Let's not be fooled, though, the white imaginary can handle the apparent contradiction. The possibility of being touched by those "gorilla hands" can, apparently, generate all sorts of white sexual fantasies.

> One white guy told me his secret [thoughts] while he was boxing . . . he always imagined his [white] girlfriend being banged by some really big black guy and this [makes him] so pissed that he could go all out in boxing.

This is the stuff of white nation building, white madness, violence, and guilt. Why doesn't he imagine *any guy*, regardless of being racialized as Black, having sex with his white girlfriend? And notice the language: she is being "banged" by him. The language is itself violent—to slam, pound, beat, hammer, batter. Out of all of the imaginative techniques at his disposal, ones that might help him to focus and knock out his opponent, it is the imagined "big black guy" that does the trick. In short, white racist fantasy, and fear of the Black body (along with the perceived, even if unconscious, "impotence" of the white male body), is what can muster and focus all of his anger and rage. Sounds all too familiar.

My friend's grandmother, while driving through a bad part of town, spotted some black people. "The neighborhood is going downhill," she sighed.

The sigh is a longing for making America great [that is, white] again, the days when Black people were not legally allowed to integrate. This is a case of white pedagogy, of passing on knowledge of those "wonderful" days when *the Blacks* were kept in their place. After all, their very presence, their Black presence, is a sign of depreciation.

Some of my friends at [university] were talking about Wiz Khalifa before our class started and the one girl made the comment that "black people have two goals in life—sell drugs or try to be a rapper."

Damn! That is so limiting. Why can't we do both? My sarcasm is fully intended. I wonder how much silence followed the white girl's comment, how the silence confirmed, within that space, the assumption about Black people.

My mom and I [were] watching "Teen Mom" on MTV and one of the girls on the show started dating a black man. My mom made derogatory comments about a white girl dating a black guy, and said that he looked like he was "no good."

This is not just an observation, but an accusation and a directive. "Darling, Black guys are really no good. Trust me." Well, let's add that they have gross "gorilla hands" and "nigger lips." But damn can they play sports and rap.

My dad and I were watching the Grammies and throughout the show there were a few different Black rap and hip-hop artists that performed. When one of the artists was performing . . . my mom said she thought that he had already performed a song and my dad said that he was pretty sure this was [a] different guy but you can't be sure because they all look the same. I just gave my dad a look and he said he was just kidding but for some reason it bothers me more when my family make[s] jokes than when my friends make jokes.

The white student should be bothered regardless. Then again, she should be *furious*. Let's face it, I'm bothered when my cat jumps in my lap uninvited. I would rather have heard that the student expressed far more outrage, though I do get the student's point. It is family, those who we trust and love. Yet there it is, front and center: all Black people look alike, one big mass of "pure, 100 percent Nigger."

I was at a house party for St. Patrick's Day and a guy walked in and greeted his friend by saying "Sup nigga" [and] then stops, looks around and says, "O good there aren't any black people here, I can say that."

This is an insult to those white people who were in fact present. There is the recognition that saying, *"Sup nigga"* is offensive. Notice how he assumes that all of the white people in earshot are fine with what he said. He holds all of them to a very low or nonexistent ethical and antiracist threshold. There is an assumption that everyone is alike.

Having read these, think about instances of backstage racism that you've witnessed or participated in. Think about the number of times that you've remained silent and thereby complicit. Also, think about what this implies for Black people who were not present—perhaps even Black friends of yours. And what does this say about the depth of the white imaginary and processes of white bonding experiences? What does this say about you as a white person?

Taking note of backstage racism can help you to engage in forms of critical listening and to unmask taken-for-granted white racism. It can also encourage new ways of thinking about complicity on your part. As a white person, you should call out your white friends and white family members on their racism. Paulo Freire writes, "Human existence cannot be silent, nor can it be nourished by false words, but only true words, with which men and women transform the world."[59] I realize that calling out your friends and family members can be very uncomfortable and risky. Indeed, it can result in the potential loss of friendships and rebuke from family members. In some cases, it can cost something as deep as the loss of show of parental love. This is where, as a white person, it is important for you to be vulnerable, to risk yourself, to expose your own white racism. Keep in mind that even the white students doing the journaling, in my view, are not free from the embedded and opaque relational dimensions of white supremacy. They, too, must remain vigilant and continue to risk themselves, to tell the truth to themselves and others. The reader should also note that this brings us back to Obama's white grandmother. The detailed familial and friendship ties in the examples of backstage racism are consistent with Obama's white grandmother's disclosures. Of course, the impact would be different given that he understood or would come to understand that he has something in common with those Black men.

What you'll most likely find is that many of those whites who you witness engaging in backstage racism are people who are generally seen to be "good people." Indeed, as Feagin writes, "What is particularly striking . . . is how the participants describe friends who do these blatantly racist performances as 'nice,' 'fun to hang out with,' or 'not a racist.' "[60] Feagin maintains that both the concept of "white virtue" and colorblind ideology, both of which are deeply embedded within what he calls a white racial frame, play a role in preventing white students from labeling as racist what is so clearly the case. Patricia J. Williams would describe this kind of reluctance to name racism as an extreme act of willful ignorance: "For white people . . . racial denial tends to engender a profoundly invested disingenuousness, an innocence that amounts to the transgressive refusal to know."[61]

If you take the necessary time and remain vigilant as best you can, you will come to realize just how much white racism occurs on a daily basis and just how much it is taken for granted. Indeed, you will come to realize just how much white racism forms the unremarkable background of your existence. As Alice McIntyre writes, "White people have grown up learning racial stereotypes that inform their thinking whether they consciously like it or not, and usually lack an awareness of the institutional racism in which they participate in every day."[62] She continues, "While in an abstract sense white people may not like the idea of reproducing white racism, and in a personal sense, do not see themselves as racist, in their talk and actions, they are."[63]

At the end of her journal for the backstage racism assignment, one white student entered a personal reflection that was unsolicited and that summarized her feelings about the assignment.

When I was given this assignment, I thought that I would have a really hard time getting journal entries, but I really have not, which was very surprising to me. Until you really listen to what people are saying and are making jokes about, you don't always realize how racist or negative the outcomes really are. This assignment really opened my eyes up to how many people I surround myself with are racist. I don't think that this means that they are horrible people, but I do think that it shows how ignorant they can be. I think that being white in America can really make someone racist without them even knowing. This is something that needs to be changed, but it will take time and effort to do that. Keeping this journal has also made me think twice sometimes about ideas in my head that I had about other people. This assignment was very eye-opening to things that I never realized were occurring around me every day.

I appreciated the honesty and insight of the disclosure. Her point about being white in America and being "racist without even knowing it" opens the door for rethinking important questions regarding whiteness, moral will, humility, opacity, embeddedness, and responsibility. And wasn't this point about being white and racist in America a core theme of Dear White America? Ignorant or not, however, one's hands are dirty, Black bodies still suffered and suffer the weight of your "innocence." As Baldwin writes, "But it is not permissible that the authors of devastation should also be innocent. It is the innocence which constitutes the crime."[64]

She also notes that she thought that she would have a difficult time, "a really hard time," getting entries for her journal. It is this assumption that hurts, that functions, whether intended or not, to mock the pervasive reality of pain experienced by Black people under white supremacy and their excruciating awareness of the ways of whiteness. And while I have no reason to doubt her honesty, it is her presumption, some might even say her impertinence, that is hard to overlook. While she is surprised, for the first time, about what she has come to discover about white people, people that she has been around her entire life, I know (and so do many Black students of the same age as she) what I am to white America.

"Nigger." That, unjustifiably, is what I am to white America. I have made that painfully clear in chapter 2. Given that dehumanizing characterization, and the hellish existence that it has caused Black people in America, *Black rage* is not unjustifiable. *My rage* is not unjustifiable. Speaking within the same affective space, Audre Lorde writes, "My response to racism is anger. . . . My fear of anger taught me nothing."[65] Rage can function as a site of being, an affect that refuses to be silenced by white racist threats, an affect that has, at times, an unbearable intensity. It is also an affect that exists alongside powerful expressions of Black joy, Black self-love, and Black ecstasy as Black people have refused to be consumed by rage, controlled by white hate, especially as we often walk near the precipice of implosion.

Within white America, Black rage is a complex affect, one fused with profound levels of *melancholy* given the harsh conditions under which Black people have had to live and endure, *weariness* given the sheer repetition of everyday anti-Black racism, and *astonishment*[66] at white America's tolerance for anti-Black racism. Saidiya V. Hartman asks, "What limit must be exceeded in order that the violence directed at the black body be made legible in the law?"[67] Although this question is raised by Hartman within the context of discussing the terrorizing institution known as American slavery, her question speaks powerfully and pertinently to our historical moment given the disposability of Black bodies by the white state, along with its proxies.

Given that Black people, the "niggers," are deemed beyond redemption, are ontologically a problem people, and apparently the paradigmatic embodiment of racialized evil and corruption, perhaps there is no limit to be exceeded. And as "law and order" function not only as tropes of whiteness, but the materializations of whiteness, Black bodies are always already sites of "unlawfulness," "chaos," and "disorder." Patricia J. Williams writes, "Culturally, blackness signifies the realm of the always known, as well as the not worth knowing."[68] She recognizes a powerful sense of irreverence implied in that white conceptual framing. She maintains that within such a context, Blackness constitutes "a space of the entirely judged. This prejudice is a practice of the nonreligious; it is profane, the ultimate profanity of presuming to know it all."[69] Then what of Black humanity? That too appears to reside within the space of the profane; it is already known; in fact, it is a circumscribed dubious category. As John T. Warren writes, "The very conception of 'humanity' in contemporary discourse is coded with whiteness."[70]

What is our option? Perhaps it is to adopt white ways, to "become white." Perhaps if we embrace the assumptions of neoliberalism, live our lives as "pre-social" individuals, atomic, self-interested and entrepreneurial, live in a state of self-denial regarding white power and privilege, and convince ourselves that America is postracial, we will become legible. Under those terms, though, I would be in a precarious and dangerous position of having denied social reality. I would have denied the deep and enduring reality of white American racism. I would quickly come to realize the fact that I can't afford to live a life of pretense. That charade will collapse once I'm pulled over by a white police officer and I'm asked to show my driver's license. Then, suddenly, there is the sound of gunshots, bullets rip through my Black body, leaving me dead, and with my last breath, while looking into the white police officer's eyes, I speak: "And I thought that I was like you—*just an individual.*" In response, many white voices will chatter, "But it was a furtive movement." Many will be relieved, knowing that "a furtive movement is a movement reasonably consistent with going for a weapon and not reasonably consistent with anything else. It is not an innocent gesture. It is a stealthy and sly movement, possibly toward a gun."[71] Add to this the white police officer's claim that he somehow "saw" a gun. Well, case closed.

My frame of reference is both historical and personal. "I almost blew you away!" Those were the terrifying words of a white police officer—one of those who policed Black bodies in low-income areas in North Philadelphia in the late 1970s—who caught sight of me carrying the new telescope my mother had just purchased for me. "I thought you had a weapon," he said. The words made me tremble and pause; I felt the sort of bodily stress, trauma, and deep existential anguish that no teenager should have to endure. This officer had already inherited those poisonous assumptions and bodily perceptual practices that constitute the white gaze. He had already come to "see" the Black male body (*my Black body*) as "different," "deviant," "dangerous." He failed to conceive, or perhaps could not conceive, that a Black teenage boy living in the Richard Allen Project Homes for very low-income families would own a telescope and enjoy looking at the moons of Jupiter and the rings of Saturn. A Black boy carrying a telescope wasn't conceivable—unless he had stolen it—given the white racist horizons within which my Black body was policed as "threatening" and "inferior." To the white officer, I was something fictional. My telescope, for him, *was* a weapon. In retrospect, I can see the headlines: "Black Teenage Boy Shot and Killed While Searching the Cosmos."[72] When I reflect on that moment as an adult, I mourn the possible death of a younger me. It is frightening to know that one's life can be taken in the blink of an eye and at such a young age. But this isn't just about mortality. This is about precious Black boys and their dreams and fantasies, ones that can cost them their lives, like twelve-year-old Tamir Rice playing with a toy gun. Then again, it is even more frightening, the affective gravitas even more intense, to know that being Black, from the perspective of whiteness, *is the problem*, that to be Black in North America is to be deemed "disposable" and "worthless"; that it is my "fate" to *make peace with a traumatized existence*, a life of mourning.

As Black, I experience my life, my Black body, as foregrounded against the background of white fabricated fears and white self-alienation. Because white people *need* me to be the criminal, the "nigger," I am doomed by either playing the role or denouncing the myth. In either case, my life can be taken away with white impunity. That is the lived and remembered trauma that I sit with: "Man, I almost blew you away!" It is the "almost" that brings actual death into closer proximity.

White reader, please know that my words here are not meant to make me into a spectacle. I am not on exhibition for you. For me, it feels as if Black embodied existence is in a constant and unrelenting state of trauma. Or, perhaps, as Claudia Rankine notes, "the condition of Black life is one of mourning."[73] Both can be true, as trauma and mourning are mutually implicative. For example, recently, a white police officer walked into a store where I was buying some food and I remember feeling this powerful sense of wanting to flee, of feeling as if the rules and laws that are designed to govern our (white) society didn't apply to me. I could move "too quickly," placing my hand into my pocket to pay for my food, and my life would end just like that. The white police officer would explain how he felt threatened and had "reasonable" suspicion. Yet, I would be dead. In short, as Rankine has suggested, because he, as a white man, can't police his own imagination, my life, and the lives of other Black men/boys are being taken.[74]

Within the store, I experienced a profound sense of fear, an embodied sense of imminent death. On other occasions, in different social spaces, while standing next to other white police officers, I have felt the shadow of death bearing upon my body. There is a palpable sense of imagining and then having my body shattered by a bullet fired from their guns. I am reminded of Elisheba Johnson's words where she writes, "A mother's love is a unique beautiful gift."[75] And yet she says, when thinking about her own

Black son, "My love isn't a bullet proof vest."[76] Given the sheer magnitude of unarmed Black bodies killed, especially Black men and boys, by white police officers and their proxies, the feeling of wanting to flee for my life, that sense of overwhelming angst, is underwritten by the contemporary expression and the historical reality of white gratuitous violence against Black people. The intense affect felt in the presence of that white police officer is *not* a case of paranoia,[77] but based upon historically grounded fear of whiteness as a site of terror. That terror or the historical promise of that terror is enough to flood one's senses with dread. That is my life white reader. Enter my world, our world, and try to see yourself as I/we see you.

ACCEPTING THE GIFT

It is important to remind you, white reader, that Dear White America was originally penned as a gift and an act of gift-giving, one informed by a profound act of vulnerability on my part. It was a gift for you that was filled with danger, though not physical violence or brutality;[1] it was/is the kind of danger that implies possibility, of being otherwise/different and not-quite-yet; it was/is a form of danger that signifies vulnerability—that is, an openness on your part to be wounded. And it is that wounding, that impairing of the structure of whiteness, that disorientation, that sense of loss of identity, and that sense of loss of pretense, that was both paradoxically the condition for hearing my voice in Dear White America and the desired harvest to be reaped after reading Dear White America.

This book, which still functions as a letter to you, is an expanded version of that gift and that act of giving. As in the original letter, I still seek to talk honestly about race. This book remains a gift that exceeds any pure self-interest on my part and any obligation on your part, as a white person, to accept it. And like the original version, this version continues *to ask* for love in return for a gift, the kind of love that derides Hollywood sentimentalism, market-driven desires that wax and wane and that keep "people in a constant state of lack,"[2] and forms of party-line loyalty that we are witnessing within our contemporary moment under Trump, that are based on cowardly sycophancy or brown-nosing. I have no use for any of that. As one reader noted in the comments section at The Stone, the *New York Times*, "The irony of the hostility in some of the comments denies the only request the author asked of the [white] reader: to read with love."

The letter is written as an entreaty with absolutely no guarantee of reciprocity. It is a solicitation that presupposes the reality of your freedom, your decision, if you so choose, to refuse the gift. I wanted, and continue to want, more than an obligation, something more than that which "binds you by oath." I was initially careful, and continue to be, because I didn't want you to act from a place of white *noblesse oblige*. I have no need of Rudyard Kipling's white imperialist rhetoric. *I am not the white man's burden*. If you are white, Black people didn't *need* you; we never asked to be treated as a burden, your burden "to save" us and "to civilize" us. I desired, and continue to desire, something greater from you; I desired to see *the real you*, the one for whom it is possible to demonstrate greater humanity and humility, a greater sense of integrity, a greater sense of genuine relationality. And despite the fact that the backlash that I received after the publication of the letter involved being called a "nigger" by white readers more times than I can recall, my gift, with no obligatory strings attached, asked more from you—a daring you, one courageous enough to risk tarrying with a disagreeable mirror that refused to walk quietly around the issue of whiteness: white supremacy and power, white privilege, and white normativity.

Yet many of you smashed the mirror of which I've previously spoken, refusing to hear me, or, as I would say, refusing to see important aspects of your whiteness. And while I realize that many mirrors do lie, some mirrors are designed to trouble you, to show you what you would rather not see. What if the *real you*, white reader, had nothing more to give than the speed with which you spewed out a name that I most certainly detest—"nigger"? Well, in that case, and in agreement with James Baldwin, "I Give You Your Problem Back. You're the 'Nigger,' Baby; It Isn't Me."[3] Don't run. Stay in the space of this transposition, this reversal. Tarry with it. As Robert Jensen writes, and I assure you that he is as white as you are, "I am a nigger, and so is every white person in the United States. . . . I am not *a* nigger, but as a white person am *the* nigger. As long as the United States remains a white-supremacist society, we can't escape this."[4] Indeed, as long as the United States remains a white governing space within which white privilege, white power, and hegemony continue to exist, and where you, as white, continue to reap the rewards, then you must ask yourself: Who and what are you and to which community do you belong? You must interrogate the ways in which you continue to contribute to my treatment as a nigger, and begin to question whether you are prepared to live a life where I am not that upon which you feed, knowingly or not. To be "eaten" by you, to be consumed by your need to be white, speaks to my real pain and suffering, and the suffering of my Black children, and Black people and people of color. It is important that you open yourself to what your whiteness extracts (*that you extract*) and to tarry with my pain and suffering and the pain and suffering of Black people and people of color such that it makes you sick, forcing a different form of relationality, one that overflows with giving.

The real question is: Are you prepared to be fully human? You should know that Jensen isn't attempting to draw attention to himself, and he certainly isn't trying to reveal his white antiracist *bona fides*. And he is certainly no white "hero." Jensen knows where to look and how to look, even as he knows that he can't, through a sheer act of will, stand outside the system of white supremacy. He writes, "For people with unearned privilege in an unjust system," and that means you, white reader, "this is the worst, to look in the mirror honestly, both to acknowledge the damage we have done to others and to see what we have done to ourselves."[5]

Just as my letter presupposed the reality of your freedom, I, too, wanted to be free to give, which is why I refused to withhold my voice, and why I openly engaged the reality of whiteness. Dear White America was never simply about me; it couldn't be. White people, you must bear in mind that an irresponsible and narcissistic expression of love belies the necessary care and concern requisite for the beloved. In such a case, there is no genuine act of gift-giving; in fact, your alterity, your otherness as the condition of being the recipient, is held prisoner. As Toni Morrison would say, within the context of such a reckless and vain expression of love, "There is no gift for the beloved. The lover alone possesses his gift of love. The loved one is shorn, neutralized, frozen in the glare of the lover's inward eye."[6] If writing Dear White America, as a letter for and to white people, can be described as an act of love, then it was never meant to be withheld, but given away— given to you, white reader.

The letter was never meant to cut you off from its invitational gesture. In the letter, I warned that some gifts can be heavy to bear. In my case, unlike Odysseus, the heroic figure in Greek mythology, who refused to risk himself, to open himself to the call of the Sirens, I, figuratively, untied the ropes that would keep me attached to the mast of the proverbial ship. So, I took a step in the water. I risked. And I certainly refused to plug my ears with wax. In fact, I refused to do so even as many of you gave me every reason to do so. Think about it from my perspective—how many times should I be expected to listen to white people call me a nigger, to take that abuse from those who look like you? To be honest, once is more than enough. As a Black person, I am no superhuman moral agent, and I'm certainly not anyone's doormat. Like you, I am broken, all too human. There is wholeness, though, that I continue to seek, an ethical and existential project that I will take to the grave.

As the giver, I, too, bore the weight of giving the gift. Think about it. I am not proud to publicly announce my sexism, though there is the seduction of taking pride in the "confession": "Yeah, I'm one of the 'good males,' one of the 'feminist conscious' ones." That, however, is a trap and I didn't fall for it. Keep in mind, as stated earlier, that I'm a male antisexist sexist (as you are a white antiracist racist). Even as I fight against sexism, patriarchal structural arrangements in our society privilege me, and patriarchal assumptions continue to impact how I see women, imagine women, arrive at certain problematic gender expectations, and conceptualize and manifest my own male bravado, my sense of male machismo. These are not inconsequential practices, but expressions of male power and violence toward women. Robert Jensen writes, "The way men talk about women and sex in all-male spaces is often brutal and cruel."[7] He continues, "The pornography produced in the United States often reflects that brutality and cruelty. Men have to come to terms with how our sexual imaginations are formed, how we are socialized to accept such inhumanity and find pleasure in it."[8]

Recall how Donald Trump clearly bragged about his treatment of women. He was recorded as saying, "Just kiss. I don't even wait. And when you're a star, they let you do it. You can do anything. Grab them by the pussy. You can do anything."[9] There we have it. There is no need to wait. This gives Nike's slogan, "Just Do It," an entirely different meaning from the one that it intends. Also recall that there were surrogates who said that Trump only *entertained* doing such things and so didn't commit sexual assault. "I don't even wait" is not something imaginatively entertained. Recall that Trump had the audacity to refer to such denigrating speech as "locker-room banter."[10] Not only is it the case that Trump admits that *he did* such things, but he attempts to diminish his misogyny by relegating what he said to the private sphere and dismisses it in a cavalier way as a noncontroversial practice among men. He also allowed Howard Stern to refer to Ivanka Trump, his own daughter, as "a piece of ass."[11] Imagine being caught using the term "nigger" to degrade Black people and then obfuscating the harm done by arguing that it was said in the privacy of his own home and dismissing it as a noncontroversial practice among white people.

Sexism and racism are no less problematic because they are performed in private. Imagine a Black male presidential hopeful having been caught talking about how he just kisses women or grabs their genitalia whenever he feels like it. And imagine if Obama had said disparaging things about white people and then tried to excuse it as said in private and therefore dismissing it as noncontroversial. He would have a snowball's chance in hell of continuing his campaign. Also, having been caught, especially as this would have implied that he was also referring to white women, imagine the blowback from white men and white women. Also, notice how Trump is the only one to blame for his comments, not *all* white men. That is white privilege. Had it been discovered that Obama said such egregious things, *all* Black men would have been demonized as bestial and hypersexual brutes. And I'm pretty sure that Obama would not have received 53 percent of the votes of all white women.[12]

Let's face it: The male pornographic imaginary pervades how I, and other men, have been inculcated to distort the erotic lives of women. We "know" how women want to be treated, what they desire, and how they ought to perform, which is not exclusive to the bedroom. This "knowing," of course, is just another way to neutralize women, to erase what the erotic means for them. For men (across "racial categories") who are reading this letter, just because I am critical of the ways in which women are objectified and dehumanized sexually does not mean that I am encouraging sexual prudery, which itself belies the embodied beauty, richness, and intensity of the erotic that I embrace. Rather, I'm arguing that it is about facing and contesting our individual and collective violence against women. It is also, as I made clear in the initial letter, about us being especially attentive to the ways in which male violence plays itself out within the context of intersectional dynamics; that is, the ways in which women, differentially located socially in terms of race, class, disability, sexuality, and gender expression, experience male violence. In the context of male hegemony, our "knowing" how women "want to be treated" is deeply problematic and narcissistic. This form of "knowing" both informs and is informed by a male pornographic imaginary. As Audre Lorde writes, "Pornography is a direct denial of the power of the erotic, for it represents the suppression of true feeling.

Pornography emphasizes sensation without feeling."[13] And contrary to the ways in which we as men have constructed women in one-dimensional ways, Drucilla Cornell speaks of women seeking a "new idiom in which we [women] can speak of feminine desire."[14] She suggests that women "not make the masculine *our* world by insisting that we 'are' only what men have made us to be."[15]

The disclosure in the letter regarding my sexism was a risk, an unmasking, as is my continued disclosure here. The powerful and instructive words of James Baldwin deserve repeating: "Love takes off the masks that we fear we cannot live without and know we cannot live within."[16] I refuse to remain silent about my complicity in the oppression of women. So, part of the objective in disclosing my sexism is to model unmasking for you, white reader; it is to demonstrate what it means to be vulnerable, which is linked to the concept of being wounded. I made myself vulnerable to you with a desire that you would reciprocate. To model in this way, though, compounds the weight to be borne, especially given the assumption that Black men and "hypersexuality" are deemed synonymous. Historically, lynching was the price paid as a result of that assumption, especially as it was believed that white women were the "preferred targets" of Black male alleged hypersexuality. Disclosing my sexism can easily be read through the lens of the myth of Black male sexual potency and the tragic consequences thereof, which can open up historical forms of painful memory associated with specific instances of Black male wounding.

Truth be told, Dear White America was always about wounding, a kind of wounding that is necessary for growth. Coming to understand the extent of my complexity with sexism is a kind of injury to the self, a wounding that I must endure; it is a type of fissure that is painful, especially as it troubles the "innocent self" that my mask portrays. There is no innocence here, whether for me as sexist or for you as racist. Well, that was at least my aim; to have us both tarry with our complicity and to admit and embrace our accountability. Of course, as the gift-giver, the Black embodied gift-giver, there was, and continues to be, a different kind of wounding, the undesirable and despicable sort that is designed to violate, to harm. I wrote the letter. It is what I had to do, but I neither expected the sheer volume of white responses nor the depravity of so many of them. In fact, I was shocked and appalled. I knew that there would be some backlash, but not white folk saying that I needed my "fucking head knocked off my shoulders," that I should be "beheaded ISIS style," that I am "100 percent pure nigger," that I am "a piece of shit," or that I would be told to "fuck off boy," or threatened with a "meat hook." Imagine what it's like to have fellow human beings say those things to you. Imagine the pain. Imagine the realization that there are actual human beings out there who believe this and who may actually be prepared to act on what they believe.

Of course, some might regard my shock as evidence of my "naiveté" regarding the wicked and inhuman treatment of Black people by white people under America's structure of white supremacy. I assure the reader that I am not naïve, but I continue to be hopeful, even as my hope feels as if it is at times complicit with white supremacy. It feels that way because as long as I remain hopeful, focusing on the future, white people can feel safe in the "knowledge" that my rage, the intensity of my affect, can be appeased by piecemeal gestures of political reform in the present. That is, I can be unmoored from the gravity of the *present* reality of my lived experience under white oppression, power, and privilege. Hope, after all, looks toward the future.

Like James Baldwin, I can't be a pessimist, because I'm alive. Yet being alive feels like borrowed time. Recall the white police officer who almost blew me away. However, I am not an optimist either, because white America is far too bleak in its ethical treatment of Black people and people of color. As such, as I continue to hope, I don't want hope to become a crutch. Perhaps what we need is a kind of post-hope, a painful recognition that as Black people we are, as you recall that Theo Shaw once said to me,[17] on death row. To be Black, in this view, is to have always already been sentenced to death in virtue of being Black within a white supremacist world, where I am just waiting to die. Post-hope is not being a pessimist or giving up in despair, rather it is a stance that we take that is more realistic. Post-hope allows one to face reality without being conned by unrealistic hope of a future that may forever be foreclosed. By the way, this doesn't speak to a metaphysical fatalism, but to the powerful recalcitrance of whiteness; its historical maintenance.

Given that this form of realism becomes ever more obvious to me, and shapes how I understand my existence and the existence of Black people within the context of white America, I ask you, white reader, to tarry within the space where I think daily about my existence and the existence of Black people within a world that privileges you. Being systemically *racially* marked for death is not a real possibility for you. Sure, it is an abstract possibility, but I'm talking about real-world possibilities with real-world consequences. Let's face it, in white America, you are not systemically *racially* marked for death. There are no historically grounded systemic practices that have marked your whiteness as a target for death. The history of Black people under white supremacist America is very different. As a white person, I want you to lose sleep over that! Become outraged! We are approaching the third decade of the twenty-first century and all that I see, all that I feel, and all that I remember tells me that so many of you don't give a damn about Black lives mattering. For now, paradoxically, I welcome the shock that I still feel when your white countrymen and women cast dispersions of racist hatred my way. In my shock, I am appalled by these racist white ways of being, but I also know that I am still open to being staggered, despite my realism, by the capacity for your demonstration of white vulnerability.

I learned an important lesson after publishing Dear White America. After I experienced so much unmitigated white hatred, I was in conversation with a prominent white public intellectual who shared with me that he had also been threatened after writing controversial articles that spoke to injustice. Through his act of sharing, I was able to appreciate our similar predicament. I felt less alienated, less alone. What became clear to me, though, is that my white colleague had not experienced *racialized trauma*. My colleague was threatened because of his exercise of courageous speech, but his whiteness remained unmarked. The objective here is not to judge who suffered more, me or my white colleague. Rather, it is important to recognize the specifically white racist hatred that I encountered; how my Black body was assaulted. My white colleague was threatened, but his whiteness was not under attack. But after the publication of Dear White America, my Blackness was assaulted. My Black body was negatively truncated and reduced to the level of the epidermis. These attacks were not only based upon what I said, but my body was the object of a white narrative that included white stereotypical assumptions, white perverse desires, white desired violence, and white hatred.

There were also other unanticipated lessons and forms of wounding. A trusted white colleague of mine said to me, after I began to receive such extreme white racist responses, that I was being disingenuous. She implied that I must have known before I wrote Dear White America that I would receive such responses. Surely, my white colleague heard me say that I had *not* expected that degree of white racist vitriol. To say that I underestimated the response is different from saying that I was being disingenuous. The latter accuses me of being deceitful. This added insult to injury. As if being bombarded with such extreme white hatred wasn't enough, I had to hear my white colleague implying that I lied. It was as if she was saying that I somehow asked for what happened. This kind of denigrating reasoning is akin to situations in which women who have been raped have been treated as having brought this on themselves: that they should have known that this would happen given what they were wearing, how they were dressed. It is perhaps easy for some white people to interpret this incident with my white colleague as one of those "less racist" incidents. However, I don't need you or my colleague to speak for me. I can speak for myself. I was the *target* of her white authoritarian denial of my epistemic integrity. As such, it is imperative that I get to define my reality, my frustration, my sense of injustice.

Dear White America challenged "white innocence." In fact, in the letter, I acknowledged that it is painful to let go of your "white innocence," to look in that disagreeable mirror that I held up to you. I know that it is difficult for you to see the ways in which you are, as discussed in chapter 3, embedded systemically within white supremacy and the ways in which your white racism is a site of opacity. As was also discussed in chapter 3, many of you said that *I am* the racist for making the claim that being white within a white supremacist society implicates you in the perpetuation of racist oppression against Black people and people of color. Given this, I discussed how this implicates you in terms of being racist, especially how you not only benefit from white racism, but that your ways of being are complicit in the continuation of white supremacy.

It may be that many of the white readers completely missed my reference to the white brothers and sisters who have made the leap, who have come to understand the relational oppressive dynamics of their white identities and what whiteness problematically means for white people in terms of *their* racism. If you missed it, I would recommend reading through the letter again. In the meantime, I will share the following examples from white scholars who have come to understand the meaning and dynamics of their white racism. John Warren writes, "I argue that I cannot escape whiteness, nor can I discount the ways I am reproducing whiteness."[18] He continues, "I agree that I cannot claim to be nonracist, to rest in the ideal of a positive racial identity."[19] Ruth Frankenberg writes, "As a white feminist, I knew that I had never set out to 'be racist.' I also knew that these desires and intentions had had little effect on outcomes."[20] That is, her white racism, whether intentional or not, still wounded women of color. Robert Jensen writes, "In a society in which white supremacy has structured every aspect of our world, there can be no claim to [white] neutrality."[21] He also argues, "It's not to pretend we all have the same political or economic power or all are equally responsible for the racialized inequality in the United States. All I am saying is no white person gets to opt out."[22] In stream with Jensen regarding the ways in which white people are positioned within the structure of whiteness, Joel Olson writes that whiteness "does not make all whites absolute equals, but that was never the intent of white citizenship."[23] Rather, the structure of whiteness, as he continues, "just ensures that no white [person] ever needs find himself or herself at the absolute bottom of the social and political barrel, because that position is already taken."[24] Within the context of white racist America, I continue to inhabit that position, and there doesn't appear to be any change of position anytime soon. Sure. I've got a PhD, but we know what that means. It means, from the perspective of whiteness, that I'm a nigger with a PhD.

I wonder what the white readers who claimed that *I* am the racist for what I wrote would say to their white brothers and sisters who understand and embrace their identities as racist and who are willing to take responsibility for their racism? Are they also "racist" (as I was labeled) because they understand how their whiteness, and yours, is integral to the maintenance of white hegemony—that is, how your whiteness functions as a site of racism? This would lead to a peculiar situation, one where white people who know that they are racists (antiracist racists), and who understand the larger institutional and historical implications of whiteness as a site of racism, are "doubly racist" because they point out the systemic and opaque dimensions of whiteness that impact and define you as racist. Then again, I imagine that there are some of you who might want to diminish what these white scholars are saying by claiming that they are "brainwashed white liberals," "white leftists," "social justice warriors," or perhaps even "nigger lovers." However, I ask that you resist that urge. I ask again that you act with love, remove the mask, don't run to seek shelter, take that leap. Drucilla Cornell writes, "The very image of the subject who strives for closure and control, rather than accept the invitation of otherness, is Odysseus as he ties himself to the mast before daring to listen to the sirens."[25]

Whiteness can be seen as a site of closure and control. When I shared the gift of seeing whiteness for what it is, I was met with denials and accusations. James Baldwin, writing to his nephew about the terrors of American white racism and how Black bodies are deemed "worthless" and are imprisoned within white institutionally condoned slums, says, "I know your [white] countrymen do not agree with me about this, and I hear them saying, 'You exaggerate'"[26] or they scream, "No! This is not true! How *bitter* you are!"[27] Such accusations of exaggeration, of bitterness, of obfuscation (like when white people called *me* a racist) function as ways of seeking shelter, claiming "innocence," and achieving closure.

I refer to these processes as ones of *suturing*.[28] I have come to use the concept of suturing within the context of understanding the structure and being of whiteness. As I see it, suturing (from Latin *sutura*, meaning a "seam" or a "sewing together") is the process whereby white people engage in forms of closure, forms of protection from various challenges to the ways in which whiteness is seen as the norm, its unremarkable everydayness, its value assumptions, and the many ways in which it's guilty about producing distorted knowledge about itself. The process of white suturing involves an effort—though I'm sure that for white people it is not recognized as an effort or as a site of active maintenance—to be "invulnerable," "untouched," "patched," "mended together," "complete," "whole," "sealed," and "closed off." To be sutured also implies a state of being free from a certain kind of "infection," which, as the reader will recall, speaks to whiteness as a site of "purity," as that which is unsullied by "difference" and "otherness." Moreover, to be sutured within the context of white identity is indicative of "the narrative authority"[29] of the white self that seals itself off from "otherness."

Dear White America, then, functioned to "contest the singularity of [your white insular] story."[30] Granted, there are many versions of the story. However, the majority of the stories converge to form a singularly agreed upon story about *me*, a Black man, having a problem, or, more accurately, about me *being a problem*. But this is a fable created by white people. Truth be told, it is whiteness that is a problem. In saying this, I am not casting nasty aspersions or name calling *because* I'm Black, but simply making a factual, historical observation. Karen Teel, a white sister, concurs. She writes, "To admit that I am a white problem is simply to state a fact."[31]

The process of suturing is also reflective of another fable: the white self as a site of self-possession and in absolute control of its own meaning. This meaning is grounded within a larger white narrative history underwritten by white power and hegemony. The sutured white self is not undone[32] by simply delineating how it has been historically constituted through relations of power. Another way of saying this is that the sutured, white imperial self's narration of its own identity tells a fantasy of "absolute" autonomy. Critically engaging and exposing the forces of heteronomy (that is, forces outside of oneself) is threatening to whiteness as the process renders visible the historically contingent struts of white normative and institutional power, which would call into question the grand gesture of white "self-creation." What I'm getting at here in terms of the day-to-day level of lived white experience is the sense in which white people take for granted the normative status of their whiteness, their white embodiment, and the ways in which in white America, for example, the white social world brings with it a whole host of moral, aesthetic, economic, and psychological advantages.

Sutured, white readers of my letter were unable and unwilling to understand any of this. They therefore reduced my voice to meaningless chatter apparently lacking epistemological, political, or moral authority. They deemed me no more than "a nigger professor." I was deemed the "racist"; I was deemed the "liar." They accused me of writing Dear White America with the ulterior motive of "hooking up with" white women. This suturing process is also conceptually linked to what Peggy McIntosh refers to as a "single-system seeing," one which "is blind to its own cultural specificity. It cannot see itself. It mistakes its 'givens' for neutral, pre-conceptual ground rather than for distinctive cultural grounding."[33] As sutured, your whiteness constitutes the fact that you have been oriented in a certain way.[34] The majority of responses that I received from white readers were founded on a certain kind of orientation, a white place from which "the world unfolds."[35] As such, then, for the majority of white readers, Dear White America was a *familiar* discursive territory; it was "a new way for me to pimp," a way for me to engage in "race baiting," a way for me to manipulate "white idiots" or a way for me to "guilt" white readers.

Yet, for me, Dear White America asked you to step out on unfamiliar discursive white ground, as it were. The letter asked that you risk your own self-understanding, to seriously trouble that white space from which the world unfolds. That is a lot to ask, but not too much when juxtaposed with the history of white terroristic threats and actual torture that Black people have experienced when they have resisted your white definition of them. I know how terrifying it must be to commit to the idea that you thought that you knew yourself only to discover that much of that was a lie, that whiteness itself is a lie. But it is really important that you know that there are some "white lies" that are not harmless, but they breed existential devastation and twisted logics of white "superiority" along with its correlative attempt to reduce the Black body to "inferior brutes." Whiteness is a profound lie that blames all social ills on Blackness. Those white lies are forms of soul sickness. Rabbi Abraham Joshua Heschel writes that racism is "a cancer of the soul"[36] and that it eats away at white people, and it metastasizes, eating away at the larger body politic and the humanity of others. Heschel writes, "The Holocaust did not take place suddenly. It was in the making for several generations. It had its origin in a lie: that the Jew was responsible for all social ills, for all personal frustrations."[37] As social ethicist Father Bryan Massingale notes:

> Racism is a soul-sickness. Racism has become a spiritual cataract; it affects what we see and what we don't see, whom we notice and whom we don't notice, and it's distorted our vision so that we don't see what's there in front of us. And body cameras and police accountability review boards, all of those are good and are necessary, but I think they're going to be limited and even ineffective if we don't realize that racism is a soul-sickness.[38]

Within the context of the white American empire, I understand what is at stake. After all, we're talking about the possible collapse of an entire white supremacist enterprise, a well-oiled machine, predicated upon acts of white world-making, where the Black body has functioned as your fixed star.[39] If not for the alacrity and desperation with which whiteness sutures itself when challenged, Dear White America would have created a powerful sense of white disorientation, perhaps even panic. You might have even lost your way, which can be a frightening experience. My letter to you, Dear White America, was written from a crucially and critically *different place*, a different site of unfolding. I tried to expose whiteness to you as something "fabulous"—that is, a fable designed to make you believe that you are special because you are white. Lillian Smith reports that of the many lessons that she learned about being white; she was taught that her "skin color [whiteness] is a Badge of Innocence which [she] can wear as vaingloriously as [she pleases] because God gave it to [her] and hence it is good and right."[40] She writes that she "clung to the belief [regarding her whiteness], as an unhappy child treasures a beloved toy, that [her] white skin made [all white people] 'better' than all other people."[41] Lastly, regarding the dos and don'ts of whiteness, Smith observes, "And we learned far more from acts than words, more from a raised eyebrow, a joke, a shocked voice, a withdrawing movement of the body, a long silence, than from long sentences."[42]

It is within the context of subtle embodied gestures that whiteness is performed, and it is through such gestures, not simply ideological falsehoods, that whiteness is perpetuated. The insidious nature of whiteness along with its "ordinariness" is a variation of what I stated in chapter 3 regarding the idea that white racism is learned at the proverbial knee. White people come to understand the meaning of those white gestures that Smith delineates as they inhabit a performative white symbolic world, a world that helps them to move about, to find their way, to orient themselves. Such a world helps to underwrite their whiteness, *your* whiteness. This is something that many of my white students have so much trouble understanding. They externalize racism as that which is flagrant, overt, and deliberate. For them, racism is something which other white people are guilty of—that is, those who openly use racist stereotypes or God forbid use the N-word. Yet a raised eyebrow from your white parents or white friends in the presence of my Black body can communicate both an entire mutually agreed upon set of white racist assumptions and an entire agreed upon repertoire of white embodied performances, even if only implicitly. That raised eyebrow, that shocked voice, that long silence, and that withdrawing movement of the body are part of a world, a site of white nation building.

The movement of white bodies within spaces at predominantly white institutions involves a dynamic set of institutional and normative forces that allow you to feel at home, for your body to move with ease. In fact, such forces extend and expand your body[43] within that space, welcoming you, and buttressing your aspirations to reach and obtain what is "rightfully" yours. There are no calculations; your white body knows how to get around. Smith asks, "What white southerner of my generation ever stops to think consciously where to go or asks himself [herself] if it is right for him [her] to go there!"[44] Smith continues, "His [her] muscles know where he [she] can go and take him [her] to the front of the streetcar, to the front of the bus, to the big school, to the hospital, to the library, to the hotel and restaurant and picture show, into the best that his [her] town has to offer its [white] citizens."[45] Similarly, Sara Ahmed writes, "White bodies are habitual insofar as they 'trail beyond' actions: they do not get 'stressed' in their encounter with objects or others, as their whiteness 'goes unnoticed.'"[46] White students are often shocked when I attempt to get them to think about white racism as a kind of habitation, which suggests a kind of structural dwelling. As Black, when I walk through that space, it begins to feel like a chair that has taken on the shape of someone else's body (in this case, your white body), a shape that is unwelcoming to my body.[47] I struggle, I squirm, while the chair resists. The chair often wins out in the end as it has been sat on for far too long by you, white reader. It has taken another's shape; indeed, your shape. That is how white spaces at predominantly white institutions feel to Black bodies and bodies of color. Within those spaces, Black bodies and bodies of color struggle, they squirm, they feel unwelcomed—they come to realize that those spaces were never *meant for them*.

Just walking while white across campus is not a racially neutral process, but a process that speaks to a racially saturated white space, historically embedded white racial power relationships, sedimentations of white normative assumptions, and a process where white bodies reap privilege and immunity for being white. I tell my white students that the simple walk between their dorm and their next class has problematic implications for my Black body and the bodies of other Black students; the bodies of Black students are impacted, touched, by white bodies whose edges don't peter out, are not discrete, but continuous. In fact, it is the *cannot*[48] of Black bodies (that is, not walking lithely across campus without that sense of being the *raced* "other") that partly involves their distress as white bodies, unstressed, move productively and smoothly across campus; it is the *can*[49] of white bodies. Like the handle on a cup, which functions as an affordance to drink from the cup, whiteness and the white normative, material, and institutional space within which white people move and have their being function as affordances that enable white students to feel at home, to be at home, as they move from room to room, building to building, to the library and back. In fact, white reader, your spaces, your campuses, are adorned with names, pictures, and statues of white people that "confirm" your membership, your racial ties, your sense of "superiority," and "specialness." White students are so braided to that white semiotic space that one of the few things that stand out for them, assuming that there is one, is the Black Student Union (BSU). In contrast, most of your unions are *de facto* white. Some of you have complained about BSUs. Yet the BSUs are not the problem. The problem is the white normative framework that makes so many white unions inconspicuous—at least *to you*.

The activity of walking across campus constitutes a site of ontological relationality that is continuous; hence, whether "passive" or "active" with respect to the perpetuation of racialized injustice, your white embodiment problematically impacts my embodiment. Vasko writes, "[White] privilege distorts privileged persons' view of reality. It tricks us [white people] into believing that we are innocent and that the suffering that befalls those on the underside of history is the result of their own inadequacies."[50] The weight and urgency of insistent interrogation and vigilance is necessary. Again, this is not about guilt, which is far too easy. "Daily [white people] should take account and ask: What have I done today *to alleviate the anguish, to mitigate the evil, to prevent humiliation*,"[51] to fight against white oppression, white arrogance, white color-evasion, white privilege, white hypocrisy, white denial, and everyday white normative ways of being?

While I briefly discussed this in chapter 3, I want to say a bit more about how I think about bodies, mine and *yours*, not petering out—that is, having no edges. Elizabeth Vasko challenges a deeply problematic conceptualization of human beings as neoliberal, atomic subjects. She writes, "To be human is to be a person in relation."[52] And Mary Elizabeth Hobgood writes, "Discerning our social location within a web of economic, political, and cultural systems is essential to evaluating our responsibility to others."[53] And Martin Luther King Jr. writes, "We are caught in an inescapable network of mutuality."[54] Along these lines, in terms of this concept of having no edges, there is something radical that I have in mind with respect to how your white embodiment fundamentally and problematically touches Black bodies and bodies of color, something that has deep ethical implications for how your being as white has deep implications for my being as

Black. This also takes us back to the notion of what it means to be yoked or "joined to." Your whiteness is always already haptic—a term that is related to *touching*. To say that white embodiment has no edges introduces what I'm calling an ontology (or being) and an ethics of no edges. In other words, an ethics of no edges and a radical rethinking of a relational ontology, where the white body does not terminate at some fictive corporeal edge, ought to encourage a different response from white people. The connection, the touching, after all, is already there. We are *now* touching each other.

An ethics of no edges that I have in mind rethinks or, better, lays bare a dynamic ontology of connectedness, a dynamic racialized somatic network (or web) that problematizes a clear-cut outside limit, and thereby calls for a robust sense of ethical responsibility, indeed, white responsibility. King writes, "Injustice anywhere is a threat to justice everywhere."[55] One way of thinking about this is that injustice is not an isolated phenomenon, but bleeds into the body politic. Heschel writes, "Whenever one person is offended, we are all hurt."[56] My point here is to encourage you, white reader, to engage critically how you are always already constituted relationally and socially and that you are politically preconfigured in the lives of Black people and people of color, especially in ways that perpetuate white racist oppression. Consistent with the idea that the structure of whiteness is one of suturing, whiteness functions as an edge. Think here in terms of white segregation, white redlining, white neighborhood covenants, and white gated communities. Such processes not only function as acts of nation building, but also the building of edges, limits, boundaries, borders, perimeters.

With this in mind, then, what are the deeper and larger implications for my act of gift-giving? Or what are the deeper and larger implications for my entreaty for an act of love from you? Within the context of whiteness, where whiteness is a site of closure, love has to be an act that troubles that "edge," that rethinks how bodies might be thought to peter out or come to an end. Perhaps a eulogy is in order. This eulogy is for the death of white forms of embodiment, conceived and lived as self-enclosed or monadic, where there is a presumed outside limit. The embodied white self, then, if it is to adopt an ethically relational ontology that troubles a white monadic identity with presumptive discrete edges, must undergo a species of death. Butler writes, "But this death, if it is a death, is only the death of a certain kind of subject, one that was never possible to begin with, the death of a fantasy of impossible mastery [and separateness], and so a loss of what one never had."[57]

In the letter, I asked that you try to un-suture. The term, as I suggest, brings to mind a state of pain, "open flesh," exposure. Un-suturing suggests processes of troubling a problematic ontology or mode of being. Un-suturing can function, within this case, as a way of undergoing a radical rethinking of the body as a site of profound vulnerability, and a radical way of being-in-the-world. White reader, I understand that there is "safety" in suturing; there is "safety" in closure. This becomes all the more understandable as your whiteness is buttressed by a conception of "purity" and a set of practices that historically have been designed to maintain your "purity," to keep you sutured from "otherness," from that which might "sully" your whiteness. Yet it is a form of "safety" that sacrifices the potential promises of difference and thereby closes off the possibility for knowing otherwise through the force of alterity. Being un-sutured, or more accurately, coming to understand how you are always already exposed, vulnerable, and open to be wounded, creates space for the ecstatic to be experienced and engaged—where your white body trembles in its contingency, openness and responsibility; where it stands in awe, where the perceptual and sensorial are shaken, unhinged.

Suturing was at work in the profiling of Trayvon Martin's body by George Zimmerman. Zimmerman, whom I shall now refer to simply as *the killer*,[58] as Martin's parents refer to him, decided to get out of his car and track down Martin. Doing discursive violence to Martin's body before the actual confrontation with him, the killer said that Martin looked "suspicious," was "up to no good," and looked like he was "on drugs," which functioned as white racist tropes that mark the Black body, that hail the Black body as a "problem body." The killer had internalized the white gaze, even though he was mixed race—his mother apparently having some Afro-Peruvian ancestry and his father of German descent. In this situation, the white gaze of the killer had already functioned as an embodied social process or vector that "touched" Martin's body. In short, this is an example of the gaze itself impacting the Black body. It actively truncates, doing violence through the ways in which it possesses the power to constitute the Black body as "deadly." The killer did not un-suture in the presence of

Martin; he did not understand how he was always already intimately entangled with Martin's Black embodiment in terms of a racially shared social skin where Martin's Black body is obstructed, stopped, distorted, touched by his white gaze and its violent history. The killer chased Martin, *pursued* him (note that "pursue" is linked to the term "prosecute," to hold a trial). It was the killer's bodily style and comportment, being on the hunt, that positioned Martin as the one who must be hunted, who is about to "commit a crime," who is to be "feared," and who is to be "tried." For the killer, Martin was disposable. The killer was on the prowl, his physical gait uninviting, his body in the mode of taking a stand. As a result, Martin's young Black body was met with a bullet, fired from a gun by a sutured self that failed to lose itself in that moment, that remained closed.

The killer sacrificed the potential promises of alterity, "otherness." For the killer, there was no place for Martin to be alive in that gated community in Sanford, Florida. After all, its edges were well defined. The racialized social space, which was predominantly white, was already touching Martin's body, structuring and configuring potential and actual racialized and racist dynamics in relationship to his Black body. In this case, the killer's white gaze had already slain the innocence and integrity of Martin's Black embodiment; the killer's white gaze had already blocked Martin's ability to move through that space with effortless grace. The killer was well sutured. There was no wonder; Martin's Black embodiment was always already *known*. There was no show of concern: "Perhaps I can help you?" There was no openness for the killer. There was no space for the killer to be surprised, for Martin "to appear to [the killer] as *new, very different* from what [the killer] knew or what [the killer] thought [Martin] should be."[59] The killer failed, refused, or just didn't give a damn to ask, *"Who art thou?"*[60] And then to say, *"I am* and *I become* thanks to this question."[61] Being and becoming presuppose a thick form of sociality that resists suturing. Within this context, *"Who art thou?"* is a question whose weight presupposes an openness, where the addressee overwhelms what we have taken for granted.

The process of un-suturing disrupts; it troubles and unsettles; it risks forms of openness or embodied gestures—un-sutured gestures that are linked to the ways in which the world reveals itself differently. Un-suturing is a form of exposure, an opening, a corporeal style and a dispositional sensibility that troubles the insularity, in this case, of the white gaze. Un-suturing troubles and overwhelms the senses, revealing how porous our bodies are and instigating instability, that sense of being thrown off balance, off center, disoriented. The killer's white gaze was not an inaugural event, but a historical formation underwritten by social hegemonic practices and white institutional forces that impact/touch Black bodies—in this case, Martin's Black body. To have become unhinged in the face of alterity/otherness/"difference," in the way that a gate designed to keep people out becomes unhinged, would have provided an opening, a fissure, and the potential for loss of orientation. Perhaps in that unhinged moment, that un-sutured moment, the killer would have lost his way, and the white hegemonic and stereotypical frame of reference operating within that space would have broken down; he would have broken down, collapsed, "fallen apart."[62] Think here of collapsing as the inability to stand, *to stand one's ground*. In that moment, it would have been the killer's white gaze that was shattered and not the life of Martin.

It is the gift of being unhinged in this way that I desired of white America when I wrote the letter. In terms of the examples of shopping while white or walking across campus as white, the very idea that your whiteness is touching me, oppressing me, truncating my humanity can result, hopefully, for you, white reader, in a fundamental process of being in deep crisis. It is such a crisis that Dear White America attempted to prompt. White reader, I wanted you to come to understand how your whiteness impacts me, touches me so that you might literally stop in your tracks as you shop or walk across campus. I desired that you might lose your way, and in so doing that you might scream aloud that you have failed to see, failed to see the damage, failed to see *me*. Imagine *screaming* that out for the world to hear.

When I say that I attempted to prompt crisis, I mean not only the sense of losing your footing, of losing your way, or a process of disorientation, but also the etymological sense of the word crisis (from Greek *Krisis*, meaning decision). Crisis, as I am using the term here, is a species of *metanoia* or conversion. This is a kind of perceptual breakdown, that is linked to the idea of that scream, that terrifying realization that your "innocence" was not real at all. Such an experience involves tarrying within that space of breakdown. It is within that space that there is a powerful sense of loss, which is actually not a loss at all, but a gain. The concept of *deciding* denotes a life of commitment to engage, perhaps every day of your life, to challenge the complex ways in which you are embedded within white supremacy and white normative structures. It is a process that will be painful and chaotic.

Indeed, it must be, because it involves facing an unfamiliar terrain; like facing the disagreeable mirror.

Perhaps you are still unconvinced. Let's try another way into this. Dear White America's message was written precisely to encourage you to risk yourself, to undergo a process of moral and existential perplexity, to rethink how your white body has come to move lithely or with effortless grace in the world. The message in Dear White America is a dangerous one, especially as it invites a dangerous undertaking. Why dangerous? As suggested previously, it involves a powerful risk. As I wrote earlier, bell hooks writes that love is about telling the truth to ourselves and telling it to others. However, for the most part, white readers of Dear White America sutured themselves, withdrew their bodies in a movement indicative of what it means to recoil. For so many white readers of the letter, there was no resulting disorientation that involved a process of truth-telling to yourself or to me or to others. You dug your heels in, sutured, and refused to accept the gift. White "common sense," as it has been constituted, spoke to you about how you're suffering in a zero-sum situation in which Black people and people of color are taking everything from you, where an inner voice whispered, "You're the victim here." My guess is that it was that inner voice that encouraged some of you to vote for Trump. Many might ask, "Do you really think that a Trump supporter is reading these lines?" Probably not. But isn't all of this about risk and the possibilities integral to that risk? Yet what if the ways in which that inner voice speaks to you about your white self is a function of a white protective discourse whose "legitimacy" is underwritten by systemic processes of white power and privilege? In this way, white power and privilege are inherent within the "self-knowledge" that you as a white person construct about yourself "and the 'wording' of [your] world."[63] And let us not forget, the structure of whiteness is predicated upon a lie. Remember, whiteness is an embodied phenomenon, a flinch, a cringe, in the presence of Black bodies and acts of Black gift-giving, especially ones that are weighty, that demand something from you.

White reader, I want you to understand how racism is not a miscalculation, or simply a cognitive distortion, but whiteness is a way of being embodied, a white way of being. It is a lie that is so intimate that *it is you*, the normative you, the you that walks into stores, attends college, and falls in love without ever asking how whiteness constitutes itself as the ground of your individual and collective white intelligibility. This is why being sutured, sewn up, is so integral to who you are as white. Being embodied as white, as a white reader of Dear White America, you refused *to cut away* at the institutional ties, the normative assumptions, and everyday white performances that seamlessly empower and privilege your white body, the ones that reassure you that as an individual your moral state depends exclusively upon your *individual* moral will, and that you are "innocent" of any racist wrongdoing. And it is important to keep in mind that that refusal to cut away at the processes of whiteness doesn't reveal itself *as a refusal* to see differently, to become otherwise, to be in danger. As so many of you read Dear White America, you clung to your whiteness as to the mast of that proverbial ship. It is that clinging, that suturing, that supports the pretense that belies bell hooks's conception of love. Suturing helps to create a false self that "has become so common that many of us forget who we are and what we feel underneath the pretense. Breaking through this denial is always the first step in uncovering our longing to be honest and clear."[64]

If whiteness is a lie, a deeply rooted historical lie, then surely who you potentially can be and how you might come to affectively engage the world differently is deferred by white norms and white embodied practices. Another way of putting this is that as partly "a constituted effect of [white] power relations and [white] intersecting discourses,"[65] you are shaped by the existence of a form of regulation of a certain "truth" about yourself not being a white person who is racist, a person whom Dear White America addressed. That brings us back to danger. Love is a kind of danger in that it requires risk, truth-telling, and honesty. James Baldwin writes, "To act is to be committed, and to be committed is to be in danger. In this case, the danger, in the minds of most white Americans, is the loss of their identity."[66]

Baldwin also writes, in words that I wish I had written, "One can give nothing whatever without giving oneself—that is to say, risking oneself. If one cannot risk oneself, then one is simply incapable of giving."[67] I risked and I gave. From all of you, I asked for you to also risk and to give—that is, to love in return. I didn't write to harm, hurt, degrade, or humiliate you, but instead to issue an alarm about your failure to confront the problem of whiteness; to cultivate a critical awareness of the specter of whiteness and white privilege that each one of you inherits. For me, knowing the history of white supremacy, its terror and hatred, my act of gift-giving was one of profound vulnerability. I took a risk to trust you, white reader. Trust is a hell of a thing. It leaves one vulnerable to attack. To know the truth of this, I ask that you revisit chapter 2. There was no risking of your white self. You didn't give of your white self. Perhaps many of you "wear so much mental make-up"[68] that you have forfeited your face. Heschel writes, "But faith [trust] only comes when we stand face to face . . . suffer ourselves to be seen."[69] Dear White America was not greeted with a *flood* of white people risking or suffering themselves (yourselves) to be seen. And relying upon Baldwin's assessment, it appears that you had absolutely *nothing to give*. To call me nigger, nigger, nigger, nigger, nigger, and then some, is *to take* as much as you can. There was no *giving*. Your response seized my humanity by the throat. And you heard my response: "I can't breathe!" "I can't breathe!" "I can't breathe!" "I can't breathe!" "I can't breathe!" "I can't breathe!" "I can't breathe!" "I can't breathe!" "I can't breathe!" "I can't breathe!" "I can't breathe!" You heard it eleven times no less.

A gift is that which is given. To give is to entrust, which means that I gave white America over to you, white reader, as something for which you were asked to take responsibility. In the end, you were rash, many of you defensive, and even more of you unconscionably vindictive and cruel, the stuff of white madness and bloodlust. Some white responses were so distorted that you might have thought that I was in a parallel universe where I was the "Black grand dragon" of the "Black Ku Klux Klan": "We can see what kind of hate is inside you. I will pray for you. You need it. All you are is a mouth piece for racism." And, "You are one of the most racist people on earth . . . your existence is kind of pathetic." And, "People pay money to get an education, instead they are subjected to assholes like you. Maybe in a few decades you will come to the realization that you are the racist." Finally, "You Vile Anti-White Motherfuckers think you've won???" There is certainly no internal battle here, no internal war against their sutured white selves. Baldwin writes, "In great pain and terror one begins to assess the history which has placed one where one is and formed one's point of view. In great pain and terror because, therefore, one enters into battle with that historical creation. Oneself."[70]

In response to my point about the necessity for an internal battle or war with one's white self, one white reader responded, "I answer that I am prepared to be at war with you, and people like you." When I speak of being at war with one's white self, it is not about engaging in acts of violence, though it will involve, by necessity, a violation, an intrusion into the safe space of whiteness, a disruption of white business as usual. It requires that you see your own nakedness, that you, white reader, un-suture, and suffer your white self to be seen. I think that a haunting is necessary for white America, one that produces ethical insomnia. That haunting is to tell the truth about whiteness to yourselves and to others so that you might know love. I'm not asking for a confession, though. Don't get distracted by the desire for absolution. Absolution runs the risk of being *all about you*. Even forgiveness can recenter whiteness, and thus obfuscate the need to explore and to interrogate your whiteness in greater depth. Confession and the desire for absolution can function as new forms of masking. I'm suggesting a haunting that Baldwin's words summon—*one can give nothing whatever without giving oneself.*

It is important to bear in mind that the act of giving oneself is neither asking me how you, white reader, can *help me* nor is it asking me to tell you how *I want* to be treated by you. The former situation reeks of white paternalism. That's a distraction, more suturing. The latter situation places the burden on me. Furthermore, who says that you are ready to hear how I want to be treated or that after hearing me you are even prepared to carry out the expressed desire? In both situations, you, white reader, emerge as the white hero, the hero who is infinitely capable of making my dreams come true, where whiteness is the answer, the solution. Yet whiteness is the problem, how you live your whiteness and its impact upon me is the problem, which means you are the problem. Begin there, begin with you, begin with telling the truth to yourself and telling it to others. Be in that place of risk, that place of danger. Tarry in that space. Don't flee. Don't wallow in guilt. And whatever you do, please don't seek recognition for just how sorry you feel. Weep if you must, but don't weep for me alone. Lament if you must, but not for me alone. Let your mourning move you to action, to fight for a world in which whiteness, your whiteness, ceases to violate me, Black people, and people of color.

Some white readers of the letter said that I had failed to offer any solutions. In fact, there were a few who seemed to say, "You say that I'm a racist, but you've provided no advice regarding what I should do." To me, this felt like another form of avoidance. I wanted, and still want, white readers to tarry within that space of profound discomfort for which the letter asks. As Ahmed would say, I didn't want to reposition you, white reader, "as somewhere other than implicated in the critique."[71] Part of the *doing* is in the tarrying, which doesn't mean navel-gazing or going off into some corner and crying in despair. I wanted you to realize that, as Heschel writes, "the history of interracial relations [in America] is a nightmare,"[72] and I wanted you to tarry with the ways in which you are complicit in supporting and benefiting from that nightmare. White reader, I wanted that letter to induce a scream from you, a refusal to live a lie, a refusal to live another day within a white supremacist system where Black people and people of color continue to be oppressed. I wanted you to suffer yourself to be seen; *to really do that.* I wanted you to tell the truth to yourselves and tell it to others, and to counter white regimes of "knowledge" production that are counter to that telling. All of this is a necessary *doing*, one that in fact outstrips the question of a specified set of tasks.

This process of necessary *doing* was undertaken by a few of your white brothers and sisters who read Dear White America. Here are some examples of what tarrying looks like, lingering with the problem and complexity of whiteness.

"I accept the gift of your letter freely and with the same spirit I believe it was intended. Thank you for your gift. I would like to offer you a gift in return: A commitment to fully accept the racism (and sexism) that is embedded in me, acknowledge the privilege that comes with having been born a white American, try my best to be educated about the suffering my racism and privilege causes others, and educate others to the extent I am able. I sincerely regret that you received hate-filled responses to your letter. I felt compelled to let you know that I, for one, don't hate you. I want to show you, and others, the unmasked, risk-taking love of which you spoke. Please accept my gift, albeit flawed, with the spirit with which it is intended. Thank you again for your work and voice on these very important matters."

"Professor Yancy's essay was breathtaking in its honesty and provocative in its pain. I am a racist, a sexist, and combat many other ills within myself that perpetuate a system that was made for me."

"Thank you. I am a white liberal/ardent backer of civil rights, but as you say, also a racist. Godspeed, and thank you for helping to keep me honest."

"Beautiful words, thoughtful words, and words that needed to be said. Thank you for holding up a mirror to my inner hate."

"Thanks Professor Yancy for your thoughts. The system is racist. As a white woman, I am responsible to dismantle that system as well as the attitudes in me that growing up in the system created. I am responsible for speaking out when I hear racist comments."

"Thank you George Yancy. You speak for me, through me, though we are different; I am a woman and white."

"Thank you, Mr. Yancy, for this gift. *I will use it every day.* Maybe some days I will be using it more adroitly, more successfully, than others, but I promise I will use it every day for the rest of my life."

"Beautiful piece in today's *Times*, Professor. I accept the difficult gift, gratefully and I hope, over time, with grace."

"Thank you for words of truth and the gift that they are."

"Dear Professor Yancy. Thank you for the letter. I am white, female, liberal and I do not consider myself a racist. What a lie! I don't use the 'N' word, I have black friends and I do the other things white liberals do so they can pat themselves on the back. Nonetheless, I recently saw a black woman walking close to my home. I wondered if she was lost and questioned in my mind what she was doing in my largely white neighborhood. The fact that this was my first thought just confirms what Professor Yancy is saying. We may think we are not racist, but many, many of us still are."

"I for one am incredibly grateful for [Yancy's] letter. In the same way that he owns his sexism, we are being invited to look inside and name and own any elements of racism that exist inside us. If you have not done this and you truly believe that there is no racism inside of you, then I gently suggest that you have not done the work that we are all here to do. I say that as a white woman. It's painful as a progressive and spiritual person to admit that there might be racism in us, but it's an integral step. I own it. And until we own and take responsibility for the racism in our own hearts, however minor, we are ignoring a hugely important part of the conversation. . . . We are being asked to see through a lens of love, and love means owning and taking responsibility. . . . That is the basis of a truly healthy relationship, and that will be the act that will heal. So grateful for this beautiful and love-filled invitation."

"I just read your opinion piece in the *New York Times*. I can honestly say it touched me, and I felt this overwhelming need to at least reach out to thank you for this gift. Speaking for myself, it made me realize the walls that I (and most likely everyone) put up every day; to cope with this confusing world, to minimize my involvement and responsibility as a human being. I hope I have the strength to be aware of my privilege and ultimate responsibility towards others on a daily basis, going forward in the New Year and beyond. Much love and respect to you and yours."

"I just read your article in *NYT*. As a white woman, I have the mirror sentiment about racism in me (the same way you have admitted sexism in you). I think we all have to start looking inwards before accusing others of 'isms.' Yes, there's racism in me, I acknowledged it and now I'm in a position to do something about it. Whether or not I succeed, I don't know, but it's a good way to start. Thank you and kudos for honesty."

"I feel that I should be on a first name basis with you because of your loving gift to me. I have been living this past year with the growing understanding that my white privilege is toxic and that I have been floating in my barge in a sea of black blood. I have sent copies of your gift to some of the people I feel closest to."

"It is a brilliant, wondrous (and sadly necessary) letter in today's *Times*. I hope that other whites will be as moved as I was reading it and truly, truly thinking about all of the implications of what you wrote."

"I just wanted to tell you that I was deeply moved by your piece in the *New York Times*. It was such an honest, accurate analysis of the problem we face in America. I found myself, almost involuntarily, reaching for the reasons I am not racist—I am married to a person of color, my child is biracial, I believe I treat all people the same regardless of their skin color. And yet, of course I know all of that is beside the point. Your piece will stick with me."

"The title of your *New York Times* article caught my eye. I read it and am trying to understand what you are hoping to accomplish. I am white, 52 years old, female and—after reading your article—willing to admit to being racist. Not **KKK** racist, not Trump racist, not ignorant and uneducated and insulated racist, but after listening with love I can admit to being racist. I am certainly the product of White Advantage: college educated father, middle class upbringing, no fear of police, etc."

"Thank you so much for your article in *the New York Times*. I've been fighting my own internal battle against racism for a little while but I still fail so miserably sometimes. I am too ashamed to describe my most recent failure. Your article and the timing of your article are truly uncanny. Your admission of your own struggles and failures are very comforting. Your language is so kind and encouraging. Your words are exactly what I needed."

"First of all, I would like to thank you for your article in the December 24th edition of *the NY Times*. I am a 53-year-old white male who has benefited from both the institutional racism and sexism you described. These thoughts have always been in the back of my mind, but were brought forth eloquently in your essay. Secondly, thank you for offering this gift during a period of time in our history in which we need this as much as ever. I will personally utilize this renewed self-awareness to be cognizant of it in my own life and in how I may positively impact it throughout the rest of my life."

"I am writing regarding your very enlightening article, 'Dear White America'. I think I get it. I am a 63-year-old, white male liberal. I suppose I have been laboring under the illusion that 'voting for Obama' and 'having a lot of black friends' lets me off the hook. Now, I see that by virtue of who and what I am, I am the problem. The racism is within me and every day of my life I am benefitting from white privilege."

"I am a 34-year-old white professional. I work and live in NYC. I have a 3-year-old daughter. I didn't really understand your article until your last paragraph: 'If you have young children, before you fall off to sleep tonight, I want you to hold your child. Touch your child's face. Smell your child's hair. Count the fingers on your child's hand. See the miracle that is your child. And then, with as much vision as you can muster, I want you to imagine that your child is black.' "

"First, I am sorry this is not a handwritten letter. Snail mail may be more meaningful, but email is an easy and environmentally friendly way to express gratitude. Thank you so much for your 'Dear White America' piece. I found it both poignant and timely. I am additionally amazed at how much it spoke to my own experience in realizing that my own feminism was distinctly white. This was an ugly moment, but realizing and embracing the constraints on my own thinking has allowed the world to proliferate with the most amazing possibilities."

"I'm sure you are getting a ton of hate mail today. I read some of the Facebook comments and they were just what you warned of. Anyway, I wanted to tell you directly what a great piece I thought it was. Just a little Christmas Eve email from this Irish girl to give you a little love back! Best wishes to you in the New Year!"

"I read your letter to White America today and wanted to thank you for your words. In the past year my eyes have been opened to real (and horrifying) racism happening all around me, but worst of all I've found it within. During the Baltimore protests in April I came across a few blogs that challenged my world view about race and every day since then I've seen America with different eyes. . . . I've seen how systemic racism is and I've seen how I benefit from that system and how I'm complicit in the oppression of people of color. As I read your letter I found myself skipping ahead, looking for the how-to section. I admit it with eyes and heart wide open that yes, your words are true, I'm racist. But, I hate it. I hate that I am an oppressor, and that I have a 2-year-old white son who could be raised to be a double oppressor."

"I wanted to thank you for your Dear White [America] piece in *the NYT*. Pretty thankless job talking to white people, trying to help us 'get' it. That 'bridge called your back.' I read some of the comments in the *Times*, but not too many. Too frustrating. I experience similar frustration trying to talk about sexism to most men—and many women. Most white people—as you know—don't see or understand the white power structures that protect and blind us. That's why they can call you racist and talk about 'reverse racism.' Anyway, thank you for making the effort. For the gift of your effort. And for using your struggle regarding sexism/patriarchy as you did. Thank you very much."

"Astounding, I was highly skeptical about this article as I read through it. I wasn't convinced that we should accept the language of white privilege and those who passively benefit from it as being an equivalent to racism. However, the last line punched me in the chest, 'I want you to imagine that your child is black.' That sold me on this argument completely, until this point I've always considered myself as extremely progressive. I've never tolerated racism, sexism, homophobia or any other form of discrimination and I always try to speak out when I see it, yet I'd never thought to consider it in that way. I felt a moment of pure shock at the sort of assumptions people would make about my child just because they were black. I can't pretend, or hide anymore. Thank you for your wonderful insight Professor Yancy."

"Thank you for this wonderful gift! I plan to pass it onto many of my friends and relatives."

"Thank you for writing this. I will hold this piece near and dear for the rest of my life. A gift indeed. Much love."

"I accept your gift and thank you."

"I wish I could memorize this!!! I want to read this every day; so encouraging! Thank you!"

"As I explore the streets and underbelly of New Orleans, the white privilege of my friends and myself is palpable. I try to live in as diverse a world as I can but here it's so evident the difference in perspective and class I have. Being a white privileged man makes me completely blind to so many realities, insulating me far beyond what I even realize. I took a long walk today overwhelmed by the differences I observed in class and color and I realized how racist I am and my belief that I'm not is pure illusion and my good intention simply isn't enough."

Perhaps for the first time, these white readers took off their masks, even if only for a moment, to hear me. Then again, perhaps they had already known about the difficulties involved in removing their masks, knowing how hard it is not to be seduced to hide, to fall back on white "innocence." They seem to have tarried in the space of danger where they dared to tell the truth to themselves and to me and to others about their whiteness. Yet as we now know, that sense of daring can easily be mistaken as white heroism. There is no place for white heroes within this book. White humility, though, is welcomed. It is such humility that "provides [white people] with an avenue to remain present to the violence done in the name of whiteness and to take up a meaningful critical stance toward that violence."[73] White heroes typically soar high above the earth. To be humble, which literally means "on the ground," speaks to the importance of engaging the muck and mire of whiteness, its everydayness, and its intractability in relationship to its social, institutional, and embodied rootedness.

These entries appear to have involved humility and risk. Your white brothers and sisters suspended pretense, perhaps only momentarily, and exposed the lie of whiteness. They un-sutured and seemed to understand that we are indeed touching. Furthermore, there was no sense of the fantasy of arrival. In other words, there was the recognition that white antiracism is a continuous and complex process, not a one-off gesture of white voluntarism. They seem to understand the concept of the nonmutually exclusive reality of the white antiracist racist. My letter did not, or so it seems, function for them as an opportunity simply to clear their conscience, to impress me with gestures of white liberal "enlightenment," or to play the role of "good whites." They appear to have looked into that disagreeable mirror and tarried within that space of white double consciousness, to have seen themselves through a consciousness not originally of their own. As stated by one white reader, "You speak for me, through me."

In the letter I revealed that I know something crucial about their opaque racist thoughts and their systemic racist embeddedness, and these readers appear to know that I know. Embarrassed? No doubt. Furious? Not obvious. However, their fury, if present, was neither directed at me nor did "they deny my right to live and be and call me misbirth."[74] There was no surreptitious effort to dance around the *problem* of their whiteness such as when people say: "I have so many Black friends whom I love. It makes my blood boil that Black lives don't matter." This kind of response suggests a sense of white self-righteousness. In contrast, for the readers I quoted, there seems to be a genuine longing to be honest and clear—even as they will falter and fail. There seems to be an act of trust. I would argue that trust presupposes fallibility, the fact that we are broken and can be broken, that we are not perfect. Yet despite this, for me, for Black people, trust, within the context of anti-Black white racism, has often been and can be far too costly. For me, white reader, especially given the historical record of white supremacy in America and around the world, trusting you is not easy. That uneasiness or downright fact of *not* trusting you at all is a problem that you have inherited and helped to perpetuate. Nevertheless, it is your responsibility to persist. Recall that this is about your demonstration of love, your vulnerability; it is about your freedom, your un-suturing, the possibility that you might become more human.

Some of your white brothers and sisters, as witnessed here, seem to have forgone that false comfort and returned the gift with love, though "not in that infantile American sense of being made happy but in the tough and universal sense of quest and daring and growth."[75] As one white reader writes, "I want to show you, and others, the unmasked, risk-taking love of which you spoke. Please accept my gift, albeit flawed, with the spirit with which it is intended." Or another, "I am a racist, a sexist." Or "Thank you for holding up a mirror to my inner hate." Or "I am white, female, liberal and I do not consider myself a racist. What a lie!" Or "my white privilege is toxic and . . . I have been floating in my barge in a sea of black blood." Or "After listening with love I can admit to being racist." Or "I am a 53-year-old white male who has benefited from both the institutional racism and sexism you described." Or "I am . . . amazed at how much [your letter] spoke to my own experience in realizing that my own feminism was distinctly white." Or "I've seen how systemic racism is and I've seen how I benefit from that system and how I'm complicit in the oppression of people of color." Or "I can't pretend, or hide anymore." Or "I realized how racist I am and my belief that I'm not is pure illusion and my good intention simply isn't enough." Or "Now, I see that by virtue of who and what I am, I am the problem."

This courage, this willingness to see yourself as the problem, *the white problem*, to see beneath the pretense, to suffer yourself to be seen, the desire to know love through the act of telling the truth to your white self and to others, of removing masks: all of that and so much more is what the gift was all about.

NOTES

INTRODUCTION

1. As a form of resistance to white supremacy, I have intentionally decided against listing these.

2. Abraham Joshua Heschel, *Abraham Joshua Heschel: Essential Writings*, ed. Susannah Heschel (Maryknoll, NY: Orbis Books, 2011), 69.

3. https://www.youtube.com/watch?v=tsKJbBb1wNA and https://www.youtube.com/watch?v=529B5F7K-RM.

4. https://www.change.org/p/american-philosophical-association-support-george-yancy.

5. https://www.change.org/p/american-philosophical-association-support-george-yancy.

6. https://www.change.org/p/american-philosophical-association-support-george-yancy.

7. 68 Scholars, "In Defense a Colleagues Facing Racist Attacks," February 25, 2016, https://www.insidehighered.com/views/2016/02/25/68-scholars-support-colleagues-column-about-race-essay.

8. Meg Wagner, "'Blood and Soil': Protesters Chant Nazi Slogan in Charlottesville," August 12, 2017, http://www.cnn.com/2017/08/12/us/charlottesville-unite-the-right-rally/index.html.

9. Yair Rosenberg, "'Jews Will Not Replace Us'": Why White Supremacists Go After Jews," August 24, 2017, https://www.washingtonpost.com/news/acts-of-faith/wp/2017/08/14/jews-will-not-replace-us-why-white-supremacists-go-after-jews/?utm_term=.c767940f92d6.

10. Frantz Fanon, *Black Skin, White Masks*, trans. Charles Lam Markmann (New York: Grove Press, 1967), 8.

11. Colleen Shalby, "From Blaming 'Many Sides' to 'Racism Is Evil' and Back Again, What Trump Has Said So Far on Charlottesville," August 15, 2017, http://www.latimes.com/politics/washington/la-na-essential-washington-updates-how-trump-s-responded-to-violence-in-1502831078-htmlstory.html.

12. Jessica Taylor, "Another Reversal: Trump Now Says Counterprotesters Also to Blame for Charlottesville," August 15, 2017, http://www.npr.org/2017/08/15/

543743845/another-reversal-trump-now-says-counterprotesters-also-to-blame-for -charlottesvi?ft = nprml.

13. Ronald Brownstein, "The NFL, Charlottesville, and Trump's Pattern of Racial Division," September 25, 2017, http://www.cnn.com/2017/09/25/politics/trump-nfl -charlottesville/index.html.

14. Bryan Armen Graham, "Donald Trump Blasts NFL Anthem Protesters: 'Get That Son of a Bitch Off the Field,'" September 23, 2017, https://www.theguardian.com/sport/ 2017/sep/22/donald-trump-nfl-national-anthem-protests.

15. Barbara Applebaum, *Being White, Being Good: White Complicity, White Moral Responsibility, and Social Justice Pedagogy* (Lanham, MD: Lexington Books, 2010), 13–14.

16. Paul Waldman, "The Privilege of Whiteness," July 22, 2013, http://prospect .org/article/privilege-whiteness.

17. The actual historical Berlin Conference (1884–1885) was one which involved major European countries dividing up and claiming territories in Africa.

CHAPTER 1

1. George Yancy, "Dear White America," The Stone, *New York Times* (December 24, 2015), https://opinionator.blogs.nytimes.com/2015/12/24/dear-white-america/ ?_r = 0.

2. James Baldwin, "White Man's Guilt," *Ebony* 20(10), August 1965, 47.

3. James Baldwin, *The Fire Next Time* (New York: Modern Library, 1962/ 1995), 7.

4. Stephanie M. Wildman and Adrienne D. Davis, "Making Systems of Privilege Visible," in *White Privilege: Essential Readings on the Other Side of Racism*, ed. Paula S. Rothenberg (New York: Worth, 2008), 114–15.

5. Robert Jensen, "White Privilege Shapes the U.S.," in *White Privilege: Essential Readings on the Other Side of Racism*, ed. Paula S. Rothenberg (New York: Worth, 2008), 130–32.

6. Baldwin, *The Fire Next Time*, 94.

7. Baldwin, *The Fire Next Time*, 94.

CHAPTER 2

1. Posted by ECO. Soul. Intellectual, "A Nigger with a PhD," July 21, 2009, http://ecosoulintellectual.blogspot.com/2009/07/nigger-with-phd.html.

2. I would like to thank Taine Duncan for this additional insight.

3. Randall Kennedy, *Nigger: The Strange Career of a Troublesome Word* (New York: Pantheon Books, 2002), 27.

4. Kennedy, *Nigger*, 27.

rde, *Sister Outsider: Essays and Speeches*, New Foreword by Cheryl
CA: Crossing Press, 1984), 40.

Angelo, "White Fragility," *International Journal of Critical Pedagogy*

, "White Fragility," 54.

s, *All about Love: New Visions* (New York: Harper Perennial, 2001), 48.

l about Love, 48.

ister Outsider, 42.

anon, *Black Skin, White Masks*, trans. Charles Lam Markmann (New
ss, 1967), 117.

aniels, *White Lies: Race, Class, Gender, and Sexuality in White Suprema-
New York: Routledge, 1997), 23.

Obama's Speech on Race," transcript, *New York Times*, online, March
://www.nytimes.com/2008/03/18/us/politics/18text-obama.html?_r=
rticle _popular&coref=slogin.

philosopher Taine Duncan for this personal communication.

Smith, *Killers of the Dream* (New York: W. W. Norton, 1949), 27.

Killers of the Dream, 29.

am Joshua Heschel, *Abraham Joshua Heschel: Essential Writings*, ed.
schel (Maryknoll, NY: Orbis Books, 2011), 68.

el, *Abraham Joshua Heschel*, 176.

el, *Abraham Joshua Heschel*, 176.

, *Killers of the Dream*, 39.

nne Rich, "Notes toward a Politics of Location," in *Blood, Bread and
ed Prose 1979–1985* (New York: W. W. Norton), 214.

n, *Killers of the Dream*, 96.

nooks, *Killing Rage: Ending Racism* (New York: Henry Holt, 1995), 31.

rt Jensen, *The Heart of Whiteness: Confronting Race, Racism, and White
an Francisco, CA: City Lights Publishers, 2005), 55.

. B. Du Bois, "The Souls of White Folk," in *W. E. B. Du Bois: A Reader*,
evering Lewis (New York: Henry Holt, 1995), 453.

Bois, "The Souls of White Folk,"453.

uld like to hear from more of my psychoanalytically trained white colleagues
nt.

iels, *White Lies*, 25.

dwin, *The Fire Next Time*, 4.

Smith, "The Dr. King We Rarely Hear About," January 18, 2010, https://
010/01/18/the-dr-king-we-rarely-hear-about/.

delle McWhorter, "Racism and Biopower," in *On Race and Racism in
Confessions in Philosophy*, ed. Roy Martinez (University Park: Pennsylvania
versity Press, 2008), 80.

would like to thank Henry A. Giroux for providing the impetus for this
.

5. Joe R. Feagin and Hernán Vera, *White Racism* (New York: Routledge, 1995), xii.

6. Feagin and Vera, *White Racism*, xii.

7. Frantz Fanon, *Black Skin, White Masks*, trans. Charles Lam Markmann (New York: Grove Press, 1967), 169.

8. Albert Memmi, *Racism*, trans with an introduction by Steve Martinot (Minneapolis: University of Minnesota Press, 1999), 175.

9. Memmi, *Racism*, 175.

10. Memmi, *Racism*, 175.

11. Memmi, *Racism*, 176.

12. Memmi, *Racism*, 174.

13. Fanon, *Black Skin, White Masks*, 173. Ronald A. T. Judy points out that the French term *nègre*, which Fanon used, has a descriptive sense as in Negro and a pejorative sense as in nigger. See Judy, "Fanon's Body of Black Experience," in *Fanon: A Critical Reader*, eds. Lewis R. Gordon, T. Denean Sharpley-Whiting, and Renée T. White (Malden, MA: Blackwell, 1996), 61.

14. I would like to thank colleague and friend Barbara Applebaum for making this important suggestion.

15. Joe R. Feagin, *The White Racial Frame: Centuries of Racial Framing and Counter-Framing* (New York: Routledge, 2010), 75.

16. I would like to thank Taine Duncan for extrapolating this point with additional clarity.

17. Kant stated, "And it might be that there was something in this which perhaps deserved to be considered; but in short, this fellow was quite black from head to foot, a clear proof that what he said was stupid." Immanuel Kant, *Observations on the Feeling of the Beautiful and Sublime*, trans. John T. Goldthwait (Berkeley: University of California Press, 1960), 113.

18. Hegel writes, "There [in Africa] they do not attain to the feeling of human personality, their mentality is quite dormant, remaining sunk within itself and making no progress, and thus corresponding to the compact, differenceless mass of the African continent." See G. W. F. Hegel, "Anthropology," from the *Encyclopedia of the Philosophical Sciences*, in *The Idea of Race*, eds. Robert Bernasconi and Tommy L. Lott (Indianapolis: Hackett Publishing Company, 2000), 40–41.

19. In *Notes on Virginia*, Jefferson writes, "Comparing them by their faculties of memory, reason, and imagination, it appears to me, that in memory they are equal to the whites; in reason much inferior." See Emmanuel C. Eze, ed., *Race and the Enlightenment: A Reader* (Malden, MA: Blackwell Publishing, 1997), 98–99.

20. David Hume, "Of National Characters," in *The Philosophical Works of David Hume*, ed. T. H. Grose, vol. 3 (London: Longman, Green, 1882) 252n.

21. The King Center (no date), http://www.thekingcenter.org/king-philosophy.

22. Stephen A. Crockett Jr., "#MakeAmericaHateAgain: 'Nigger' Spray Painted on Home Owned by LaBron James," May 3, 3017, http://www.theroot.com/makeamerica hateagain-nigger-spray-painted-on-home-own-1795694861.

23. I first discussed this horrible situation in a chapter titled "The Violent Weight of Whiteness: The Existential and Psychic Price Paid by Black Male Bodies," in *The*

Oxford Handbook of Philosophy and Race, ed. Naomi Zack (New York: Oxford University Press, 2017).

24. Fanon, *Black Skin, White Masks*, 112.

25. Fanon, *Black Skin, White Masks*, 114.

26. Fanon, *Black Skin, White Masks*, 116.

27. The Mary Turner Project (no date), http://www.maryturner.org/.

28. Judith Butler discusses vulnerability and precariousness in her book, *Precarious Life: The Powers of Mourning and Violence* (New York: Verso, 2004). I will return to these concepts in chapter 3.

29. James Baldwin, *The Fire Next Time* (New York: Modern Library, 1962/1995), 96.

30. Butler, *Precarious Life*, especially chapter 2.

31. Joel Kovel, *White Racism: A Psychohistory* (New York: Columbia University Press, 1984), xliv.

32. Kovel, *White Racism*, xlv.

33. Fanon, *Black Skin, White Masks*, 180.

34. Cornel West, *Race Matters* (Boston: Beacon Press, 1993), 86.

35. Fanon, *Black Skin, White Masks*, 158.

36. The reader should note that such white racially distorted frames of reference also shape Black police officers and police officers of color in terms of how they come to interpret Black bodies. In short, the white gaze is mobile.

37. Joe R. Feagin, *Racist America: Roots, Current Realities, and Future Reparations* (New York: Routledge, 2010), especially chapter 4.

38. Fanon, *Black Skin, White Masks*, 167.

39. David Levering Lewis, ed., *W. E. B. Du Bois: A Reader* (New York: Henry Holt), 454.

40. Lewis, *W. E. B. DuBois*, 454.

41. bell hooks, *Killing Rage: Ending Racism* (New York: Henry Holt), 46.

42. Judith Browne Dianis, "Eric Garner Was Killed by More Than Just a Chokehold," August 5, 2014, http://www.msnbc.com/msnbc/what-killed-eric-garner.

43. Lenzy Krehbiel-Burton, "Oklahoma Deputy Who Killed Eric Harris Found Guilty of Manslaughter," April 29, 2016, http://www.huffingtonpost.com/entry/oklahoma-deputy-who-killed-eric-harris-found-guilty-of-manslaughter_us_57239339e4b0b49df6ab2d4f.

44. David A. Graham, "The Mysterious Death of Freddie Gray," April 22, 2016, https://www.theatlantic.com/politics/archive/2015/04/the-mysterious-death-of-freddie-gray/391119/.

45. Ray Sanchez, "Laquan McDonald Death: Officer Indicted on 16 New Charges," June 27, 2017, http://www.cnn.com/2017/03/23/us/laquan-mcdonald-case-hearing/index.html.

46. Rafael A. Olmeda and John Marzulli, "Unarmed Amadou Diallo Is Killed by Four Police Officers Who Shot at Him 41 Times in 1999," February 5, 1999, http://www.nydailynews.com/new-york/unarmed-amadou-diallo-shot-killed-police-1999-article-1.2095255.

47. Charlie Leduff, "What Killed 2010 issue, http://www.motherjones.co

48. Jason Hanna and Amanda Watts 1 Suspended," May 30, 2017, http://w -police-officers-disciplined/index.html.

49. *Black Voices*, "Renisha McBride While Trying to Get Help, Family Says post.com/2013/11/06/renisha-mcbride-d

50. Gerald C. Hynes, "A Biographica http://www.duboislc.org/html/DuBoisBio.

51. A brilliant thinker, friend, and one the Jena Six in Jena, Louisiana.

52. Henry A. Giroux, *Disposable Youth: elty* (New York: Routledge, 2012), 36.

53. Brad Evans and George Yancy, "The 18, 2016, https://opinionator.blogs.nytin -black-philosopher/.

54. Feagin, *The White Racial Frame*, 104

55. Feagin, *The White Racial Frame*, 104.

56. Holly Yan, Kristina Sgueglia, and Kyl Hate Speech and Crimes Post-Election," *CN* .com/2016/11/10/us/post-election-hate-crimes

57. Kovel, *White Racism*, 189–90.

58. Eric Anthamatten, "Trump and the Tr https://www.nytimes.com/2017/06/12/opinior .html?rref=collection%2Fcolumn%2Fthe-stor opinion&region=stream&module=stream_u =5&pgtype=collection.

59. Stephen Greenwald, "The Real Politicia April 10, 2017, http://www.huffingtonpost.com/ -of-a_b_9649954.html.

60. Michael M. Grynbaum, "Trump Tweets a Ground," July 2, 2017, https://www.bostonglobe. -tweets-video-that-seems-show-him-attacking-cnn WDL/story.html.

61. Robin DiAngelo, "White Fragility," *Intern* 3(3) (2011): 57.

62. James Baldwin, "White Man's Guilt," *Ebon*

63. https://www.youtube.com/watch?v=Ua2Rb

CHAPTER 3

1. James Baldwin, *The Fire Next Time* (New Yo 80.

2. Audre L
Clarke (Berkeley
3. Robin D
3(3) (2011): 54
4. DiAngelo
5. bell hook
6. hooks, *A
7. Lorde,
8. Frantz
York: Grove Pr
9. Jessie D
*cist Discourse (
10. "Barack
18, 2008, http
1&incamp=a
11. I thank
12. Lillian
13. Smith
14. Abrah
Susannah H
15. Hesch
16. Hesch
17. Smith
18. Adrie
Poetry: Selec
19. Smit
20. bell
21. Robe
Privilege (S
22. W.
ed. David
23. Du
24. I w
on this po
25. Da
26. Ba
27. Jef
griid.org/
28. La
America:
State Un
29. I
expressio

30. Peggy McIntosh, "White Privilege and Male Privilege: A Personal Account of Coming to See Correspondences through Work in Women's Studies," in *Critical Whiteness Studies: Looking behind the Mirror*, ed. Richard Delgado and Jean Stefancic (Philadelphia: Temple University Press, 1997), 293–94.

31. McIntosh, "White Privilege and Male Privilege," 298.

32. Zeus Leonardo, *Race, Whiteness, and Education* (New York: Routledge, 2009), 75.

33. Barbara Applebaum, *Being White, Being Good: White Complicity, White Moral Responsibility, and Social Justice Pedagogy* (Lanham, MD: Lexington Books, 2010), 29.

34. Applebaum, *Being White, Being Good*, 30.

35. Applebaum, *Being White, Being Good*, 28.

36. Stephanie M. Wildman and Adrienne D. Davis, "Making Systems of Privilege Visible," in *White Privilege: Essential Readings on the Other Side of Racism*, ed. Paula S. Rothenberg (New York: Worth, 2008), 114–15.

37. Robert Jensen, "White Privilege Shapes the U.S.," in *White Privilege: Essential Readings on the Other Side of Racism*, ed. Paula S. Rothenberg (New York: Worth, 2008), 130–32.

38. Cynthia Kaufman, "A User's Guide to White Privilege," *Radical Philosophy Review* 4(1–2) (2002): 32.

39. bell hooks, *Talking Back: Thinking Feminist, Thinking Black* (Boston: South End Press, 1989), 113.

40. I use this term in the philosophical spirit of Judith Butler, particularly in terms of its poststructural implications, though I restrict its use here to speak to white subject formation.

41. Judith Butler, *Precarious Life: The Powers of Mourning and Violence* (New York: Verso, 2004), 26.

42. Barbara Applebaum, citing Zeus Leonardo, "Flipping the Script . . . and Still a Problem: Staying in the Anxiety of Being a Problem," in *White Self-Criticality beyond Anti-Racism: How Does It Feel to Be a White Problem?* ed. George Yancy (Lanham, MD: Rowman & Littlefield, 2015), 5.

43. Applebaum, *Being White, Being Good*, 158.

44. Iris Marion Young, *Global Challenges: War, Self-Determination and Responsibility for Justice* (Malden, MA: Polity Press, 2008), 175.

45. Edward S. Casey, "Walling Racialized Bodies Out: Border versus Boundary at La Frontera," in *Living Alterities: Phenomenology, Embodiment, and Race*, ed. Emily S. Lee (Albany: State University of New York Press, 2014), 190.

46. Applebaum, *Being White, Being Good*, 179.

47. McIntosh, "White Privilege and Male Privilege," 292.

48. Applebaum, *Being White, Being Good*, 46.

49. Barbara Trepagnier, *Silent Racism: How Well-Meaning White People Perpetuate the Racial Divide* (Boulder, CO: Paradigm, 2006), 15.

50. https://www.youtube.com/watch?v=529B5F7K-RM.

51. Ann Berlak, "Challenging the Hegemony of Whiteness by Addressing the Adaptive Unconscious," in *Undoing Whiteness in the Classroom: Critical Educultural Teaching Approaches for Social Justice Activism*, eds. Virginia Lea and Erma Jean Sims (New York: Peter Lang, 2008), 55.

52. Judith Butler, *Giving an Account of Oneself* (New York: Fordham University Press, 2005), 79.

53. Tim Wise, *White Like Me: Reflections on Race from a Privileged Son* (New York: Soft Skull Press, 2005), 133.

54. Wise, *White Like Me*, 133.

55. Joe R. Feagin, *The White Racial Frame: Centuries of Racial Framing and Counter-Framing* (New York: Routledge, 2010), 124.

56. Thanks to Barbara Applebaum for encouraging me to emphasize this point.

57. Richard Wright, *Eight Men* (New York, Harper Perennial, 1996), 213.

58. James Baldwin, "White Man's Guilt," *Ebony* 20(10) (August 1965): 47.

59. Paulo Freire, *Pedagogy of the Oppressed*, 30th Anniversary Edition (New York: Continuum International Publishing Group, 2000), 88.

60. Feagin, *The White Racial Frame*, 126.

61. Patricia J. Williams, *Seeing a Color-Blind Future: The Paradox of Race* (New York: Farrar, Straus and Giroux, 1997), 27.

62. Alice McIntyre, *Making Meaning of Whiteness: Exploring Racial Identity with White Teachers*, Foreword by Christine E. Sleeter (Albany: State University of New York Press, 1997), xi.

63. McIntyre, *Making Meaning of Whiteness*, xi.

64. Baldwin, *The Fire Next Time*, 5.

65. Lorde, *Sister Outsider*, 124.

66. Of course, given the history and brutality of white supremacy, there is little that leaves Black people in a state of astonishment.

67. Saidiya V. Hartman, *Scenes of Subjection: Terror, Slavery, and Self-Making in Nineteenth-Century America* (New York: Oxford University Press, 1997), 81.

68. Williams, *Seeing a Color-Blind Future*, 74.

69. Williams, *Seeing a Color-Blind Future*, 74.

70. John T. Warren, "Performing Whiteness Differently: Rethinking the Abolitionist Project," *Educational Theory* 51(4) (2001): 458.

71. Ben Findley, "A Furtive Movement Can Get You Killed," December 6, 2013, https://www.usacarry.com/furtive-movement-get-you-killed/.

72. See the longer version of the article in which this example is discussed: George Yancy, "Walking White Black in the White Gaze," September 1, 2013, http://opinionator.blogs.nytimes.com/2013/09/01/walking-while-black-in-the-white-gaze/.

73. Claudia Rankine, "The Condition of Black Life Is One of Mourning," June 22, 2015, http://www.nytimes.com/2015/06/22/magazine/the-condition-of-black-life-is-one-of-mourning.html?_r=0.

74. See https://www.youtube.com/watch?v=kugyV79R_io.

75. Elisheba Johnson, "A Love Poem for Michael Brown," in *Our Black Sons Matter: Mothers Talk about Fears, Sorrows, and Hopes*, eds. George Yancy, Maria del Guadalupe, and Susan Hadley (Lanham, MD: Rowman & Littlefield, 2016), 139.

76. Johnson, "A Love Poem for Michael Brown," 139.

77. I share with my students that given the historical context of white racism in America, I ought to be petrified in the company of all white people. This doesn't mean that white people don't experience dread in the company of Black people. Yet, and this is important, we have to ask about the origins and function of that dread. The long history and contemporary manifestations of white supremacy undergird my dread; there is no comparable legacy of Black antiwhite violence that undergirds white dread.

CHAPTER 4

1. But keep in mind that Dear White America was met with the threat of violence, with violent speech. Thus, I risked a great deal. I would like to thank Karen Teel for making this point explicit.

2. bell hooks, *All about Love: New Visions* (New York: Harper Perennial, 2001), 47.

3. https://www.youtube.com/watch?v=My5FLO50hNM.

4. Robert Jensen, " 'You're the Nigger, Baby, It Isn't Me': The Willed Ignorance and Willful Innocence of White America," in *White Self-Criticality beyond Anti-Racism: How Does It Feel to Be a White Problem?*, ed. George Yancy (Lanham, MD: Rowman & Littlefield, 2015), 88.

5. Jensen, " 'You're the Nigger, Baby, It Isn't Me,' " 99.

6. Toni Morrison, *The Bluest Eye* (New York: A Plume Book, 1970), 205.

7. Robert Jensen, *The Heart of Whiteness: Confronting Race, Racism, and White Privilege* (San Francisco, CA: City Lights Publishers, 2005), 73.

8. Jensen, *The Heart of Whiteness*, 73.

9. Ben Mathis-Lilley, "Trump Was Recorded in 2005 Bragging about Grabbing Women 'by the Pussy,'" October 7, 2016, http://www.slate.com/blogs/the_slatest/2016/10/07/donald_trump_2005_tape_i_grab_women_by_the_pussy.html.

10. David A. Fahrenthold, "Trump Recorded Having Extremely Lewd Conversation about Women in 2005," October 8, 2016, https://www.washingtonpost.com/politics/trump-recorded-having-extremely-lewd-conversation-about-women-in-2005/2016/10/07/3b9ce776–8cb4–11e6-bf8a-3d26847eeed4_story.html?utm_term=.60e7a6e8ed0a.

11. Laura Bassett, "Donald Trump: Sure, Call My Daughter a 'Piece of Ass,' " October 8, 2016, http://www.huffingtonpost.com/entry/donald-trump-ivanka-ass_us_57f9553ae4b0b6a43032d9a0.

12. Katie Rogers, "White Women Helped Elect Donald Trump," November 9, 2016, https://www.nytimes.com/2016/12/01/us/politics/white-women-helped-elect-donald-trump.html.

13. Audre Lorde, *Sister Outsider: Essays and Speeches*, New Foreword by Cheryl Clarke (Berkeley, CA: Crossing Press, 1984), 54.

14. Drucilla Cornell, *Transformations: Recollective Imagination and Sexual Difference* (New York: Routledge, 1993), 105.

15. Cornell, *Transformations*, 105.

16. James Baldwin, *The Fire Next Time* (New York: Modern Library, 1962/1995), 94.

17. See chapter two of this book, note 51.

18. John T. Warren, "Performing Whiteness Differently: Rethinking the Abolitionist Project," *Educational Theory* 51(4) (2001): 465.

19. Warren, "Performing Whiteness Differently," 465.

20. Ruth Frankenberg, *The Social Construction of Whiteness: White Women, Race Matters* (Minneapolis: University of Minneapolis Press, 1993), 3.

21. Jensen, *The Heart of Whiteness*, 17.

22. Jensen, "'You're the Nigger, Baby, It Isn't Me,'" 89.

23. Joel Olson, *The Abolition of White Democracy* (Minneapolis: University of Minneapolis Press, 2004), 29–30.

24. Olson, *The Abolition of White Democracy*, 30.

25. Cornell, *Transformations*, 44.

26. Baldwin, *The Fire Next Time*, 7.

27. Baldwin, *The Fire Next Time*, 5.

28. George Yancy, "Introduction: Un-Sutured," in *White Self-Criticality beyond Anti-Racism: How Does It Feel to Be a White Problem?*, ed. George Yancy (Lanham, MD: Rowman & Littlefield, 2015).

29. Judith Butler, *Giving an Account of Oneself* (New York: Fordham University Press, 2005), 37.

30. Butler, *Giving an Account of Oneself*, 37.

31. Karen Teel, "Feeling White, Feeling Good: 'Antiracist' White Sensibilities," in *White Self-Criticality beyond Anti-Racism: How Does It Feel to Be a White Problem?*, ed. George Yancy (Lanham, MD: Rowman & Littlefield, 2015), 22.

32. Judith Butler, *Precarious Life: The Powers of Mourning and Violence* (New York: Verso, 2004), 23.

33. Peggy McIntosh, "Interactive Phases of Curricular and Personal Re-Vision with Regard to Race," Working Paper #219 (Wellesley College Center for Research on Women, 1990), 1.

34. Sara Ahmed, "A Phenomenology of Whiteness," *Feminist Theory* 8(2), 152, 2007.

35. Ahmed, "A Phenomenology of Whiteness," 151.

36. Abraham Joshua Heschel, *Abraham Joshua Heschel: Essential Writings*, ed. Susannah Heschel (Maryknoll, NY: Orbis Books, 2011), 66.

37. Heschel, *Abraham Joshua Heschel*, 177.

38. Gretchen R. Crowe, "Unpacking the 'Soul-Sickness' of Racism," July 13, 2016, https://www.osv.com/OSVNewsweekly/Article/TabId/535/ArtMID/13567/ArticleID/20273/Unpacking-the-soul-sickness-of-racism.aspx.

39. Baldwin, *The Fire Next Time*, 8.

40. Lillian Smith, *Killers of the Dream* (New York: W. W. Norton, 1949), 89.

41. Smith, *Killers of the Dream*, 90.

42. Smith, *Killers of the Dream*, 90.

43. Ahmed, "A Phenomenology of Whiteness," 153.

44. Smith, *Killers of the Dream*, 96.

45. Smith, *Killers of the Dream*, 96.

46. Ahmed, "A Phenomenology of Whiteness," 156.

47. Ahmed, "A Phenomenology of Whiteness," 163.

48. Ahmed, "A Phenomenology of Whiteness," 161.

49. Ahmed, "A Phenomenology of Whiteness," 150.

50. Elisabeth T. Vasko, *Beyond Apathy: A Theology for Bystanders* (Minneapolis, MN: Fortress Press, 2015), 131.

51. Heschel, *Abraham Joshua Heschel*, 74. Of course, Heschel's concern here exceeds white supremacy and speaks to all the ways in which each of us has failed to fight on behalf of others, to relieve their pain and suffering.

52. Vasko, *Beyond Apathy*, 220.

53. Mary Elizabeth Hobgood, *Dismantling Privilege: An Ethics of Accountability* (Cleveland, OH: Pilgrim Press, 2009), 33.

54. Martin Luther King Jr., *A Testament of Hope: The Essential Writings and Speeches of Martin Luther King, Jr.*, ed. James M. Washington (New York: Harper-SanFrancisco, 1991), 290.

55. King, *A Testament of Hope*, 290.

56. Abraham Joshua Heschel, *Abraham Joshua Heschel: Essential Writings*, ed. Susannah Heschel (Maryknoll, NY: Orbis Books, 2011), 69.

57. Butler, *Giving an Account of Oneself*, 65.

58. Sybrina Fulton and Tracy Martin, *The Enduring Life of Trayvon Martin: Rest in Power, A Parents' Story of Love, Injustice, and the Birth of a Movement* (New York: Spiegel & Grau, 2017), 44.

59. Luce Irigaray, *An Ethics of Sexual Difference*, translated by Carolyn Burke and Gillian C. Gill (Ithaca: New York: Cornell University Press, 1993), 74.

60. Irigaray, *An Ethics of Sexual Difference*, 74.

61. Irigaray, *An Ethics of Sexual Difference*, 74.

62. George Yancy, *On Race: 34 Conversations in a Time of Crisis* (New York, NY: Oxford University Press, 2017), 61–71. I thank philosopher Alison Bailey for the critical discussion regarding what it means for white people to, as she says, "fall apart."

63. Alecia Youngblood Jackson, "Performativity Identified," *Qualitative Inquiry* 10(5) (2004): 676.

64. hooks, *All about Love*, 48.

65. Jackson, "Performativity Identified," 680.

66. Baldwin, *The Fire Next Time*, 8.

67. Baldwin, *The Fire Next Time*, 85.

68. Heschel, *Abraham Joshua Heschel*, 185.

69. Heschel, *Abraham Joshua Heschel*, 185.

70. http://www.douglasficek.com/teaching/phil-4450-phil-of-race/baldwin.pdf.

71. Ahmed, "A Phenomenology of Whiteness," 165.

72. Heschel, *Abraham Joshua Heschel*, 70.

73. Rebecca Aanerud, "Humility and Whiteness: How Did I Look without Seeing, Hear without Listening?" in *White Self-Criticality beyond Anti-Racism: How Does It Feel to Be a White Problem?*, ed. George Yancy (Lanham, MD: Rowman & Littlefield, 2015), 111.

74. W. E. B. Du Bois, "The Souls of White Folk," in *W. E. B. Du Bois: A Reader*, ed. David Levering Lewis (New York: Henry Holt , 1995), 453.

75. Baldwin, *The Fire Next Time*, 94.

INDEX

ABOUT THE AUTHOR

George Yancy is professor of philosophy at Emory University. He is the author, editor, and coeditor of over eighteen books. He is known for his influential essays and interviews in the *New York Times'* philosophy column, The Stone. He resides in Atlanta, Georgia.